FRIENDS IN WILMINGTON
1738–1938

Friends in Wilmington
1738–1938

Published by Your Legacy Press.
www.yourlegacy.press

2st edition, January 2016

For permission to copy or share this work, please write:

Wilmington Friends Meeting
401 N. West Street
Wilmington DE 19801-2730

Ordering Information at www.createspace.com/6002013
or at www.amazon.com

ISBN-13: 978-0692623985
ISBN-10: 0692623981

Book design by Mary Helgesen Gabel, Your Legacy Press. www.yourlegacy.press.

This printing is a reproduction of the first printing in 1938. Images and content pages were scanned from the original book. A preface was added and the table of contents was typeset.

Printed in United States of America.

Sunshine and Shadow

MEETING HOUSE INTERIOR, FOURTH AND WEST STREETS · 1938

PREFACE

When, in 1938, Wilmington Monthly Meeting of the Religious Society of Friends celebrated its 200th anniversary, the Meeting set up a Bicentennial Committee to organize a commemoration of the event. This committee then organized a smaller Book Committee and tasked it with publishing *Friends in Wilmington: 1738–1938*. In 2014, a concern was raised that few copies remained of this informative book and that some members and attenders were unfamiliar with the Meeting's history. In response, the Meeting decided to republish the book as part of its celebration of the 200th anniversary of the building of Wilmington Meeting's current Meeting House, in which Friends in Wilmington have worshiped since September 25, 1817.

This slim volume, the result of the work of Friends in 1938–39, is rich in historical content. Essays, some of which were presented at Bicentennial events, provide the history of early Delaware Quakerism, Quaker education in Wilmington, especially at Wilmington Friends School, and Friends' philanthropic work. Two of its essays address well-known men associated with the Meeting, John Dickinson, the "Penman of the Revolution," and member Thomas Garrett, abolitionist and stationmaster on the Underground Railroad. The 1938 bicentennial celebrations are described and include the text for the Meeting's "Historical Pageant" that was presented at Wilmington Friends School's then-new location in Wilmington's Alapocas neighborhood. Completing the volume are various lists that document the Meeting during the eighteenth and nineteenth century: membership, marriages, burials, as well as genealogical information of early Meeting families whose descendants remained active members in 1938. And distributed throughout are maps, poems, and photographs that provide other means to understand and reflect on Wilmington Monthly Meeting's history.

As the Meeting approaches the 200th anniversary of worshiping in its current Meeting House, we are pleased to honor those who worshiped here before us by republishing this volume of our early history. We are thankful that earlier Friends had the foresight to create this spiritual oasis and to faithfully maintain it. Though much has changed within our Meeting House and in the surrounding Quaker Hill neighborhood during the intervening years, each First Day we continue to worship in expectant silence for the leadings of the Spirit. We trust that both as individuals and as a community we will continue to be led by our testimonies of simplicity, peace, integrity, community, equality, and stewardship as we meet the current and future challenges of the twenty-first century.

AT FRIENDS MEETING

Sunshine and shadow o'er unsculptured walls
  Hang tremulous curtains, radiant and fair;
  The breath of Summer perfumes all the air;
Afar the wood-bird trills its tender calls.
More eloquent than chanted rituals,
  Subtler than odors swinging censers bear,
  Purer than hymns of praise or passionate prayer,
The silence like a benediction falls.
  The still, slow movements softly slip along
  The endless thread of thought; a holy throng
Of memories, long prisoned, find release.
  The sacred sweetness of the hour has lent
  These quiet faces, calm with deep content,
And one world-weary soul alike, the light of peace.

—Susan Marr Spalding
Wings of Icarus, 1892

THIS BOOK IS DEDICATED
TO THOSE NOBLE MEN
AND WOMEN OF THE
QUAKER FAITH WHO
HAVE BY EXAMPLE AND
PRECEPT BUILT FOR US
A WAY OF LIFE.

EXPLANATORY NOTES

Meeting For Worship.-A stated or regular, specially appointed, occasional, or private assemblage for Divine Worship.

Particular Meeting.-A stated or regular meeting, held in most cases twice a week.

Preparative Meeting.-Formerly, corresponding to each stated meeting for worship the local members were constituted also as a Preparative Meeting, for matters of local concern or for the preparation of business for their Monthly Meetings. Two or more Preparative Meetings constituted an administrative body, the **Monthly Meeting.** Preparative Meetings have been discontinued except where holding of title to property, administration of funds, etc. necessitate them.

At the present time the organization consists of **Monthly** (meeting once a month), or **Executive Meetings,** in which membership is recorded and which report to Quarterly (sitting four times a year), or Half-Yearly Meetings; second, **Quarterly** and **Half-Yearly Meetings,** consisting of one or more Monthly Meetings which report to the Yearly Meeting (sitting annually); third, the **Yearly Meeting,** comprising all the above Meetings.

A meeting is **set up** when an assembly is given permission by an established Meeting to conduct Stated Meetings, and is **laid down** or discontinued by permission of a similar authority.

Women's Meeting.-Formerly the men and women in an assembly were seated at opposite ends of the meeting room. Some physical barrier such as a railing or movable partition to mark this division is found in most of the older meeting houses. This distinction was carried also into the business activities of the organization and led to the establishment of Men's Meetings and Women's Meetings. When both meetings were called at the same time the movable partition was closed between the two groups. These customs, together with many others once common among Friends, have gradually disappeared and the business affairs of the Meeting are now conducted by a single group of men and women.

FOREWORD

THE committee entrusted with the compiling of this book has found its task a pleasant one. We have chosen to present considerable historical material of the factual type and to tell the story of Friends in northern Delaware as it has been written into ancient and in most cases unpublished records. Of the generations now living we have said but little. Their contribution to history is not yet complete.

In the Roll Call are the names of those whom many now living remember as friends and relatives rather than as historical characters. The date 1900 has been chosen arbitrarily in dividing the past from the present generations. Comments concerning any individual are limited to the listing of official contributions to the Meeting or to an intangible something so well recognized as to be traditional.

The Genealogies are limited to those of early Quaker families in Wilmington whose descendants are now members of the Meetings. They do not include the generations whose members are still living.

In the history of the Meeting and of Friends School are recorded events of recent date. Those who follow us will wish through such records to picture the environment, customs and philosophy of the year 1938.

We are happy to present among our illustrations recent pictures of the neighboring meeting houses. These are the material emblems of a group of meetings of the same parentage (Newark Monthly Meeting) as our own. To these meetings, our older sisters, we extend greetings.

For purpose of record, there have been given the names of the general committees in charge of the Bicentennial Celebration and the names of those who played the parts of historical characters in the pageant. We wish it were possible to give credit by name to the more than three hundred Friends and friends of Friends who labored so effectively to make the Bicentennial Celebration a most satisfying occasion.

Of the general committee, the Book Committee was a part. Contributions to the book have come from many sources. It relates the story of Friends in Wilmington as told by Friends. We are grateful for the generous cooperation of the Pennsylvania Historical Society, the Historical Society of Delaware, the Friends Historical Association, Haverford College and Swarthmore College.

For the Committee
Edward P. Bartlett

CONTENTS

Illustrations

   The inscription reads—"laid down at 200 ft. in an Inch the 27th day of
August An. Dom. 1777—per Jacob Broom, Surv. N'Castle Co'y." The
distances are recorded in "M" (miles) "q" (quarter miles) and "pr" (perches
or rods). The map was prepared at the request of George Washington. Some
of the notes on the map are in his handwriting. The names showing the
locations of the Friends Meetings are recent additions. The original map is
the property of the Pennsylvania Historical Society.

THE QUAKER MESSAGE

Esther Smedley Chambers

S IN all religious movements, the Society of Friends has been maintained by principles or beliefs. The principle that George Fox called "that of God in every man," was to him a living experience, a faith that God continually reveals His love through the Eternal Christ or "Inner Light" in men's lives. This truth is one of the greatest contributions that Friends have offered to the world. Another contribution has been the "way of life," which Quakerism in its very inception attempted to find,—a way of life that cannot separate the religious and the secular, for all that one does must be for the glory of God. It is living the Christ-like life each day in one's relationship with God and with man. Religious thought and interpretation have varied through the years, but these basic principles of Quakerism not expressed in any formal creed, but deeply rooted in the lives of its members, have persisted and become the life of the Quaker movement.

Quakerism in its form of worship is founded on this philosophy of life. Since God endows every man with a measure of His Divine Spirit, man may communicate directly with God. In worship, the communion and baptism of the Spirit may be known without any outward symbols. Silence is one of the best preparations for this meeting of man with God. No outward authority can replace the dictates of a soul following the Divine Light. In this fellowship of silence, when the soul touches the Infinite, God's word may be revealed to every man at some time, and expressed through vocal ministry. In such a silence and with such a ministry the Meeting for Worship may be "like the rising of the water in a lock which enables the ship to go out for its journey on a higher level."[1]

The Quaker testimony on peace is based on this principle of the Divine in every man. The solution of the world's conflicts is fundamentally a spiritual one. No peace based solely on social and economic adjustment can be lasting. Unless we can feel peace in our hearts towards the individual or the nation, as George Fox said, "Live in the

---

[1] Rufus M. Jones

Spirit that taketh away the occasion for war," intellectual and economic arguments are futile. It is through reconciliation rather than denunciation that real peace can be achieved. Hatred, greed, jealousy and fear must be replaced by love and understanding. We know the answer that Jesus gave the young lawyer when he asked how to inherit the eternal life. The first commandment, "Love thy God," had its counterpart in the second, "Love thy neighbor." Men are still asking "Who is my neighbor?" Is not the parable of the Good Samaritan still the answer?

Quakerism in its outward expression through service is based also upon these same principles of man's inherent endowment of the "Divine Spark," and this seeking for a "way of life." Economic, racial, and international justice can be founded only upon this ideal. The Friendly way of life means being a friend to every man regardless of creed, color, class or country. It means pioneering in the field of social service,—a service that includes both clothing men's bodies and feeding their souls.

In Education also, is found this same central unifying principle. The "way of life" is a search for a more abundant life. Quaker Education is founded on the belief that spiritual growth must keep pace with mental and physical growth. It is developing personal character, learning to live in fellowship with others, and giving oneself in service. Habits and attitudes are as essential as skill and knowledge. Humanizing interests when related to life's purposes enlarge one's scope and vision. "Quaker Education is a religion at work, both redemptive and remedial, redemptive for the individual and remedial for society."[2]

Thus in Education, in Service, and in Worship, the message of Quakerism has not changed in its three hundred years of history. It is for each generation, in the light of existing conditions, to relive and reinterpret this message through men's lives. The Friends World Conference, conscious that Quakerdom awaited some solution of the world's problems, closed with this thought, "The most vital message of the Society of Friends is the Spiritual Messenger. He, the Eternal Mystic Christ and Inner Light, sent, not by us, but by our Father into every soul, will use our hands, our words, our every power, if we offer them unreservedly." The Quaker message rests upon the consecrated individual member. He is the apostle and through him alone shall Quakerism live.

---

2 John A. Lester

THE BEGINNINGS OF QUAKERISM
IN DELAWARE

Alice A. Johnson

THE story of the settlement of Friends in the Three Lower Counties on the Delaware is rich in romance and adventure, frequently accompanied by stern hardships that tested to the utmost the living faith which Friends possessed.

These early settlers came in great numbers. History states that during the year 1681 alone twenty-three English ships, with emigrants to the province, arrived in the Delaware. There was no ocean greyhound with its advertised four day voyage but rather the "John and Sarah," the "Bristol Factor" or the "Kent" setting forth toward an unexplored world over seas tempestuous and almost uncharted. After a voyage of eight weeks or more, arriving in an unknown harbor, the adventure frequently turned into a calamity. Such befell the "Bristol Factor" when it arrived in Chester Creek, where it flows into the Delaware. The passengers, seeing some houses, went on shore, at Robert Wade's Landing, and the river freezing during the night held captive both boat and passengers for the winter. But the "Amity," having been blown off its course clear to the West Indies, did not arrive until the Spring.

However, the earnest seeker for religious freedom was not discouraged by such mishaps nor by the wild country with its primeval forests, the unbridged rivers, the paths or trails along which the red man made his excursions, the bogs and swamps and the animals such as those against which the Court at New Castle legislated when it ordered setting fifty-two "wolfe pitts or trap houses." Here and there along the water courses were lonely farm houses and occasionally small groups of houses where lived the Dutch, Swedes and Finns.

A census, taken about 1661, showed that "Swedes, Finns and other nations" had over a hundred farms stocked with cattle, horses, sheep and swine. Fort Casimir and the town New Amstel with about one hundred houses, was the metropolis of the Delaware and the seat

(13)

of government for the territory below Christina. Altena or Fort Christina was the seat of government for the northern part, and Governor Stuyvesant had appointed Sir William Beeckman, commissary or vice Director for South River, which included all the forts, villages and farms. It was about a quarter of a century since the arrival of the Swedes, and it was to be at least three-quarters of a century more before a Quaker Meeting was established in Wilmington.

However, Quakers already had plantations in Maryland and other parts of the New World as indicated by the following quotation from Ward's "The Dutch and Swedes on the Delaware 1609-64": "One stray English Quaker, a certain 'Captain Voeler' whose name in his own tongue was probably Wheeler, came to Altena in 1661. He was a refugee from Maryland. Beeckman, vice Director, was much concerned about him, stating that he showed 'not the least respect' to the Director, and he 'was aware of his defect of manners,' but said 'his conscience did not allow it.' 'Whereupon I answered,' says Beeckman, 'that our conscience could not tolerate such a persuasion or sect. If he keeps still and no more followers of that sort shall arrive, I shall tolerate him, but in case of increase I shall make him leave our jurisdiction pursuant to the praiseworthy orders made by your Honorable Worships, the Director and Council at New Amsterdam.'" Evidently Captain Voeler did not attempt to "set up" a Quaker Meeting at Altena, but many other Friends were colonizing the New World, and in 1671 George Fox had a concern to visit America. It was in that year George Fox wrote to his wife, who was imprisoned in England for her religious beliefs. "I wrote to her to acquaint her, that it was upon me from the Lord to go beyond sea, to visit plantations in America . . . I had finished my service for the Lord in England, the ship and the friends that intended to go with me, being ready, I went to Gravesend the 12th of 6th mo. 1671." Delayed by storms and a tempestuous voyage, "The third of the eighth month, early in the morning, we discovered the island of Barbadoes, having been seven weeks on the high seas. After a visit of three months or more in Barbadoes—I found drawings to Jamaica—We were between six and seven weeks in this passage from Jamaica to Maryland—We began our journey by land to New England, a tedious journey through woods, wilderness, bogs and great rivers, passing over or through rivers, Tredaven, Miles, Wye, Chester and Saxifrax, being obliged to lie in the woods several nights—finally reaching a Dutch town called

New Castle." But he did not tarry there at that time. "We departed thence and got over the river Delaware, not without great danger to some of our lives. Through a wilderness since called West Jersey, not then inhabited by English—on to Middletown, East Jersey, and then to Oyster Bay, Long Island, to attend the half yearly meeting which lasted four days."

In returning South, for he and his party set sail for England from Maryland, he planned as he expressed it, "to pass through the woods on the other side of the Delaware-bay, that we might head the creeks and rivers as much as possible—The ninth of the seventh month (1672), we set forward, passed through many Indian towns, and over some rivers and bogs. When we had rid about forty miles, we made a fire at night and lay by it. As we came among the Indians, we declared the day of the Lord to them. Next day we traveled fifty miles as we computed; and at night finding an old house, which the Indians had forced the people to leave, we made a fire and lay there, at the head of Delaware-bay. The next day we swam our horses over a river about a mile, at twice, first to an island called Upper Dinidock, and then to the mainland, having hired Indians to help us over in their canoes. This day we could reach but about thirty miles and came to a Swede's house were we got a little straw and lay that night. Next day, having hired another guide, we travelled about forty miles through the woods and made a fire at night by which we lay and dried ourselves, for we were often wet in our travels. Next day we passed over a desperate river, which had in it many rocks and broad stones, very hazardous to us and our horses. From thence we came to Christian-river, where we swam our horses over and went ourselves in Canoes, but the sides of the river were so miry that some of the horses had like to have been laid up. From thence we came to New Castle, heretofore called New Amsterdam; and being very weary, and inquiring in the town where we might buy some corn for our horses, the Governor came and invited me to his house, and afterwards desired me to lodge there; telling me he had a bed for me, and I should be welcome. So I staid, the other friends being taken care of also. This was on seventh day, and he offering his house for a meeting, we had the next day a pretty large one; for most of the town were at it. Here had never been a meeting before, nor any within a great way; but this was a very precious one, many were tender, and confessed to the truth, and some received it; blessed be the Lord forever." A remarkable testimony and an extra-

OLD KENNETT MEETING HOUSE

CENTER MEETING HOUSE   *Photos by J. Edgar Rhoads*

ordinary portrayal of the wilderness through which George Fox passed, but in which he discerned the possibilities of a haven for sore-pressed Friends.

Thus on the fourteenth of September, 1672, at New Castle, in the Harmony Street house of Governor Lovelace, the first Quaker meeting in Delaware, and a "very precious one," was held by none other than George Fox himself, and thus was Quakerism brought to Delaware.

It is interesting to note that the "desperate river—hazardous to us and our horses" was the beautiful Brandywine Creek, usually so peacefully rippling over those "many rocks and broad stones." John Russell Hayes in his poem "The Brandywine," sang of the peace of the river:

> "How many happy hearts have thus been led
> . To close communion with earth's lovely forms,
> Beloved Brandywine, and who would not
> Record with grateful voice the debt of joy,
> Of pure unfading joy and rapture high
> Whose first awakening he owes to thee."

Before the arrival of William Penn in 1682, great strides had been made in establishing means of communication with the different settlements, as indicated by the following court order at New Castle in 1679: "the highways to be cleansed as followeth, viz. The way be made clear of standing and lying trees, at least ten foot broad, all stumps and shrubs to be cut close by ye ground. The trees marked yearly on both sides, sufficient bridges to be made and kept over all marshy, swampy and difficult dirty places, and whatever else shall be thought more necessary about ye highways aforesaid." It was about this time that Cornelius Empson was granted the privilege of establishing a ferry across the Brandywine. Previously, the traveler could choose between wading and going over on horseback. The ford was an Indian trail and was used long before the coming of the white man. Later it became a road, but it was 1762 before a bridge was built at the "falls," probably at French Street.

Perhaps the first Friend to settle in this vicinity was Thomas Wollaston, who in 1667, 1668 and 1669 bought land in New Castle County: White Clay and Mill Creek Hundreds.[1]

Ezra Michener in his book on Early Quakerism,[2] states that "about the year 1682 several families of Friends arrived and settled on the east side of the Brandywine in New Castle County." One Valentine Hollingsworth, who came to America in 1682, obtained a patent for land which he called New-Wark. He was a member of the Society of Friends and meetings were held at his home. The following account quotes freely from Edward W. Cooch's paper on Valentine Hollingsworth and his family. Valentine Hollingsworth came to America the same year as William Penn, who sailed from Deal, a seaport of England, not far from Dover, August 30, 1682, on Board the ship "Welcome," landing at New Castle on October 27th. Penn granted to Valentine Hollingsworth and members of his family tracts of land in his "Manor of Rocklands." In 1688 several inhabitants of the Manor of Rocklands petitioned Penn for grants of marsh land (for pasturage) in the proportion of ten acres of marsh for each one hundred acres of upland. Hollingsworth was a member of the first assembly of the Province of Pennsylvania 1682-3; also of the Grand Inquest empaneled October 25th, 1683, to consider the famous case of Charles Pickering and others charged with counterfeiting. He was a Justice of the Peace from New Castle County, a signer of Penn's Great Charter and a member of the Pro-Provincial Council. William Stockdale in his ' Great Cry of Oppression" tells that year after year in England, Valentine Hollingsworth like other Quakers, refused to pay tithes for the support of the State Church, and how just as regularly the tithe mongers confiscated great quantities of his barley, oats, hay, wheat and corn. In America the sincerity of his faith is shown by the organization of the New-Wark meeting as well as his gift of land for a burial place. A brief account of some of those who cooperated with Valentine Hollingsworth in the founding of New-Wark meeting follows. Morgan Druet (Drewett) a mariner, was the first of the founders to come to America, having arrived from London, with his wife Cassandra, at Burlington, New Jersey, in 1677, in the ship "Kent." Early the next year he purchased land in Marcus Hook where he resided until 1681 at which time he removed to a large tract of land on the river just above "Boute Creek." By the establishment of the circular boundary of Delaware his property was located in New Castle County, and it was at his house meetings for worship were held. He served as juror at the first court held under the Proprietary Government.

Thomas Conway was a son-in-law of Valentine Hollingsworth, having married his eldest daughter Mary.

Cornelius Empson, who established the ferry mentioned previously was a Justice of the Peace. In that capacity he was one of those having supervision of the survey. He served five times in the Provincial Assembly.

William Stockdale was a minister in the Society of Friends and traveled throughout the country carrying his message of truth. He migrated with his wife to America about 1687, and was instrumental in securing a grant of land for a meeting house in New Castle County. His wife having died soon after their arrival, he married in 1689 Hannah Druet, daughter of Morgan and Cassandra Druet. Stockdale was a member of the Provincial Council 1689-1690 from New Castle County.

From early accounts and from the records in the Minutes of the Newark Monthly Meeting 1686-1739, the history of the Friends Meetings from the first meeting held by George Fox at New Castle in 1672 to the founding of the meeting in Wilmington in 1738 can be traced with considerable accuracy.

The first entry in the minute book of the Newark (New-Wark) Monthly Meeting is of no particular interest except that it is the first entry and shows that another English Quaker had wandered north from Maryland.

3rd mo. 7th, 1686—"At the monthly meeting held at Widow Welsh's, Edward Gibbs and Judith Crawford proposed their intention of marriage with each other, ye man producing a certificate from ye monthly meeting in Maryland and signifying his clearness." "Widow Welsh" probably was the widow of William Welsh who represented New Castle County in the Provincial Assembly until his death in 1684.

11th mo., 1686—"At our monthly meeting at ye Widow Welsh's at New Castle, Robert Turner and Susanna Welsh proposed their intentions of marriage with each other, ye man producing a certificate from the monthly meeting at Philadelphia signifying his clearness, ye woman's mother being present, gave her consent, a certificate from London being produced signifying her clearness during her residence there."

Can this Robert Turner be the Robert Turner who was one of Penn's most trusted friends, and who is described in the Colonial

HOCKESSIN MEETING HOUSE

STANTON MEETING HOUSE   *Photos by J. Edgar Rhoads*

Records as one of the wealthiest and most prominent merchants of the Philadelphia of that day? He it was who built the first brick house in that city as well as a wharf called "Mount Wharf" on his lot facing the river. From Albert Cook Myers' book "Quaker Arrivals at Philadelphia, 1682-1750" the following is noted: "Robert Turner and family from Men's meeting in the City of Dublin dated 5/3/1683. He being an 'antient' Friend of this Meeting—a 'widow man'." In the minute quoted below his substantial subscription rather lends color to the supposition.

Even at this early date the group of Friends meeting together at Widow Welsh's saw the need for care of the indigent and the following minute is recorded: "The meeting consented to subscribe, as it shall be in ye freedom of each friend, towards a public stock for ye relief of ye friends in necessity. Cornelius Empson, 5 (shilling), Edward Blake 4, William Gregg 5, Valentine Hollingsworth 5, John McCombs 5, John Richardson 5, Robert Turner 15, Thomas Snelling 2."

In 1938 the distance in miles between New Castle and New-Wark (Carrcroft) in Brandywine Hundred is quickly and easily covered but two and one-half centuries ago the rocky Brandywine, the miry Christina, the trails over which slow travel was necessary made many problems for the early Friends. Consequently the following minutes seem entirely justifiable.

11th mo. 7th, 1687—"The Monthly meeting being held at Morgan Druetts, it is ordered by friends at this meeting that the monthly meeting is to be held at Valentine Hollingsworth's for ye convenience of friends living on ye other side of Brandywine, and ye first day following the meeting to be there likewise, till farther consideration— Valentine Hollingsworth hath freely given unto friends for a burying place half acre of land for ye purpose, there being some already buried in ye spot. Friends have deferred fencing of it till ye next meeting." At the monthly meeting held at Valentine Hollingsworth's 10th mo. 7th, 1689, "George Harlan desiring ye concurrence of friends on behalf of ye families on ye other side of Brandywine for ye holding of a meeting this winter season amongst themselves by reason of the dangerousness of ye ford, to which meeting agrees and consents."

In less than a score of years growth of the meeting necessitated more permanent or larger quarters, or perhaps a more central location. The monthly meeting ordered, 3rd month 1704, "that the next monthly meeting be held at Center, which is supposed to be George Harlan's 'Ould House'." George Harlan, with his brother Michael, came from the north of Ireland about 1687, and in settling in the vicinity seemed to assume a position of importance in the deliberations of the meeting. In the latter part of 1706 the monthly meeting at Center appointed Cornelius Empson, George Robinson, George Harlan and Thomas Hollingsworth, son of Valentine, who was full of years, to meet and consult together about building a meeting house. Subscription lists, items of purchase and hauling of timber and payment of the "sawyers" are all noted in the minutes.

In 1708 the meeting appointed George Harlan, Alphonsus Kirk, Samuel Greaves, and Thomas Hollingsworth, to agree with workmen in order to build a meeting house, the dimensions forty feet long by twenty feet wide. In 1710 the minute records that "Alphonsus Kirk is to be allowed 7s. 6d. per acre for the land the meeting needs not to exceed 6 acres." The meeting house was built at Center which is about one-half mile east of the present Centreville.

There seems to be no record of the exact date of the first meeting in New Castle, although Friends met together as early as 1683. The Philadelphia Quarterly meeting first month, 1684, records the following minute: "This meeting being acquainted that some friends and friendly people in and about New Castle does desire that a meeting for the worship of God every first day may be held among them. The which the meeting considering, are well satisfied that of some be appointed, having Unity with them in the same. The meeting also ordered that friends of New Castle be acquainted with the same." Widow Welsh, Edward Blake, John Richardson and others were hospitable and opened their homes, but the need for a building in which to worship was appreciated by the Friends and the Newark monthly records show these early efforts to obtain such a house; dated 2nd mo. 7th, 1688—"Friends having taken into consideration ye necessity of building a Meeting House and to have some land for ye same to stand on; therefore by ye agreement of Friends of ye meeting, William Stockdale is desired to endeavor to get a grant for some land for ye same when he goeth next to Philadelphia, in some convenient Place in ye Governors Mannor." The following month, 3rd mo. 6th, at the quarterly meeting held at Edward Blake's at New Castle, the meeting "appointed a First-day meeting weekly at the said Edward Blake's, and four persons to view a place for a meeting house and graveyard." Edward Blake and John Richardson were members of the Provincial Council and the former was Justice of the Peace of New Castle.

Apparently the removal of the monthly meeting to the "other side of the Brandywine" did not meet with the approval of the Friends in New Castle. This may have been due partly to the condition of the road, but more possibly to their interest and time being centered in erecting a meeting house for themselves. That they were several times requested to attend the monthly meeting at Newark or Center is noted in the extract of 1689 from the meeting records. "The meeting being held at Morgan Drewitt's, debated concerning the deficiency of Edward Blake and others, belonging to the meeting at New Castle, in not answering the desire of this meeting by coming hither on this side of the Brandywine Creek, but have notwithstanding absented themselves. The meeting therefor appointed that the next Quarterly meeting be held this side of the Brandywine where it will fall in course. Adam Sharpley and Thomas Connaway were appointed to acquaint Friends at New Castle with the reasons for removing Quarterly meeting from thence at this time."

It was in seventh month, third, 1720, that a board of Trustees was appointed consisting of John Richardson, Nicholas Meers, George Hogg, Jr., and Edward Gibbs, "to take conveyance of the meeting house and grounds in New Castle from the Heirs and Executors of Benjamin Swett and John Hussey, Senior, for the Service of the people called Quakers, to them their heirs and assigns."

"Nicholas Meers," according to an unpublished Manuscript of Benjamin Ferris, "was one of the early settlers in Wilmington. He lived on the hill long known by the name of Quaker Hill in a house which formerly stood on a lot next above Smith's boarding school on West Street and when he died between the 16th of 9 mo. and 11th of 11th mo. in the year 1761, age 111 years, his body was interred in Friends burying ground near his residence. The ground now occupied by Pasture Street (the present Washington Street) was then partly included within the grave yard. About that time the Society of Friends had concluded to bury promiscuously in rows all who should thereafter die, excepting only such who had previously adopted family plots. Meers was the first without a family plot who died after that word and his body was buried in the north corner of the yard which since the widening of Pasture Street is in a spot outside the wall."

Title was obtained to a plot of ground, one hundred and twenty by three hundred feet on Beaver and Otter Streets (now Fourth and Fifth) in New Castle. Here stood the small plain meeting house with the plot behind it serving as a burial ground, and here gathered the few Friends on First and Fourth days to worship in their simple manner. In 1752 John Richardson deeded the property to another Board of Trustees consisting of Benjamin Swett, John Lewden, Joseph Lewden, Eliakim Garrettson, and Joseph Rotheram under whose care the meeting for worship continued until 1763 when it was finally "laid down" while the members attended at Wilmington, the property passing into the possession of the latter meeting. Old records show that the Meeting house was used for a school building in 1779. To quote from the pamphlet "Development of Education in New Castle," by Richard S. Rodney: "In that year George Read, Nicholas VanDyke and David Finney rented for school purposes, from John Lewden and others the then Trustees, the Meeting House of the Society of Friends. They paid £6 per annum for the use of the building." The monthly meeting records of 3rd mo. 13th, 1799 give a minute as follows: "Nicholas Robinson and Jacob Starr having requested to be released from the care of the meeting house at New Castle is concurred with and Isaac H. Starr, John White, Joshua Johnson are appointed to pay the further necessary attention thereto." A few years later the question of burial in the graveyard arose; a committee was appointed to give thought to the matter and reported 8th mo. 9th, 1804 "that in future it will be proper not to admit interments in that ground, without a permit first obtained from the committee who stand appointed for that service, and they, as applications are made, are desired to exercise a judicious care therein." The placing of stones over the graves provoked discussion and action, for in the same year a minute of the Wilmington Monthly Meeting records: "It being the sense of this meeting that such stones should be removed, the Committee appointed to the care of that meeting house and burial ground are desired to use their endeavors with the connections of those deceased persons, where stones are so placed, to have them removed."

A steady stream of immigration had set in following William Penn's visit in 1682 and some of the settlers around White Clay Creek, commonly called Whitely Creek, petitioned in sixth month, 1687, the monthly meeting at New Castle for permission to hold a weekly meeting at Whitely Creek. This was granted but apparently there was

LONDON GROVE

NEW GARDEN

some question in the minds of the members, for at the monthly meeting tenth month, 1687, "Cornelius Empson and Henry Hollingsworth were ordered to go to Whitely Creek and see what order their meeting is in." Again at the quarterly meeting following: "Edward Blake and George Harlan were ordered to give the meeting at White Clay Creek a visit and see what order they are in and also to signify to some of them the care of this meeting concerning them and to make a report at the next monthly meeting." Alas! Only too true—the meeting was discontinued second month, seventh, 1688 and those Friends who desired "to worship in Truth" attended the New Castle Meeting. Almost a century later, in 1772, meetings for worship were held at White Clay Creek on First and Fourth days at the various homes, namely at Hannah Lewden's at Christiana Bridge or at Samuel Reynold's or at William Marshall's Mill. This was only a temporary arrangement for in 1779 "the meeting was removed from William Marshall's Mill to a new house built for a school house which this meeting (Concord Quarterly) approves of." It was at this time "the meeting produced a lease from Thomas Stapler to Robert Johnson, Robert Philips, Joseph Chambers, William Wollaston, and William Byrnes, in trust for a piece of land whereon their meeting house stands, dated the thirteenth day of sixth month, 1779." This lease recorded in 1786 in Deed Book F. Vol. 2, page 268, states: "For the said people called Quakers to bury their dead in and to build upon; they the said Johnson et al trustees, their heirs and executors yielding and paying to the said Thomas Stapler, his heirs and assigns the yearly rent of pepper corn, on the thirteenth day of the sixth month each year forever; if demanded, and to make and keep fences in good order around said land." In 1803 White Clay Creek Preparative Meeting requested a change of name from White Clay Creek to Stanton. The meeting house now standing was built about 1872 replacing the earlier one built about 1780.

Settlements were now rapidly extending westward and requests for additional places of worship are frequently noted in the minutes of the monthly meetings at Center, Newark or Kennett, for these meetings seem to be interchangeable.

In 1709, Howell James requested that consent be given Friends in and about "ye Iron Hills" for a meeting once a month at Howell James' house. In some of the minutes, this location is referred to as "Elk River."

In 1713, Friends at New Garden petitioned the monthly meeting that Friends of the meeting kept at John Miller's might build a meeting house. This was granted with the stipulation that it be within a half mile of Michael Lightfoot's. Michael Lightfoot and his wife Mary Newby came to New Garden with the Irish Immigrants in 1712. In 1743 he removed to Philadelphia to take the post of Provincial Treasurer, an office he held until his death in 1754.

The New Garden settlement was a part of Stenning Manor, the plantations, two hundred to one thousand acres each, being purchased from William Penn, Jr., by Friends who emigrated from the "Kingdom of Ireland" in 1712.

In 1714, Friends in the western part of East Marlborough requested that a meeting be settled at the house of John Smith, one First-day in every month and every Sixth-day for half a year. This meeting later became London Grove.

In 1717, Friends asked for advice from the Quarterly Meeting for settling a place to build a new meeting house for Kennett. Within two months the committee, Thomas Bradshaw, Josiah Fearne, William Lewis, Aaron Jones, Henry Osbourn and John Bezer reported their choice of location as: "That part of Vincent Caldwell's land that lies betwixt the two roads that go to Nottingham and into the woods."

In 1719, Friends in the Forks of the Brandywine requested "that a meeting for worship be granted every other First-day and every other Fifth-day." This later became Bradford Meeting.

In 1730, Friends in Mill Creek Hundred requested to have a week day's meeting settled amongst them and the following were appointed "to give them a visit and make a report of their sense concerning the request"—Abraham Marshall, Thomas Wickersham, Potter Collings, and Ellis Lewis. In response to this request of Friends of Mill Creek, "liberty was granted to keep a meeting at the house of William Cox upon the sixth day of the week every week until further order." In 1738 the Mill Creek Friends were given permission to build a meeting house at Hockessin. This building is incorporated in the present structure, the alterations and additions being made in 1745. Meeting is held in this building every First-day.

Eleventh month, seventh, 1737, at the Monthly Meeting of Newark held at Kennett, the following minute is recorded: "Newark Preparatory meeting acquaints this meeting that our Friends of Wilmington desire to have a meeting of worship settled amongst them on First days and week days which is referred to the next monthly meeting for consideration." At the next monthly meeting, twelfth month, fourth, 1737, the request of the Friends of Wilmington was granted and referred to the Quarterly Meeting. A few days later, the thirteenth, the Concord Quarterly Meeting received the following representatives for Newark: Ellis Lewis, Thomas West, David Ferris, and Christopher Wilson. At this time a minute was presented from Newark Monthly Meeting on behalf of Friends living in or near Wilmington requesting liberty to keep meeting for worship First and Fifth-days. In 1738 "Newark Preparative Meeting refers to the consideration of this meeting (Newark monthly) Thomas West for the elder of Wilmington meeting, Joseph Hewes and William Warner over seers of said meeting which this meeting approves of til further orders."

Eighth month, sixth, 1739—Wilmington Friends requested a preparative meeting and the following were appointed as a committee to visit them and report: Ellis Lewis, Samuel Greave, William Levis and Thomas Carleton. The next month the minute records that "they think it may be of service, therefore ye said request is to be laid before ye Quarterly Meeting for approbation," which request was granted.

Twelfth month, second, 1739—Wilmington Preparative Meeting "signifies the desire of Zachariah Ferris being joined to this meeting and also to have the privilege of our meetings of Discipline, which is granted." At the same meeting a request was made that John White might have the privilege of sitting with the ministers and elders in their meeting; William Shipley and Jacob Chandler were appointed to inquire into his conversation and ministry and report to the next meeting.

In 1749, "Wilmington and New Castle preparative meetings renew their former requests of the liberty of having a monthly meeting settled amongst them, therefore we appoint William Pennock, Thomas Carleton, Swithin Chandler, Joseph Maddock, William Harvey, and Samuel Levis to give them a visit at their preparative meeting as they may think most proper and report at the next meeting."

A record made twelfth month third, 1749—"Our next monthly meeting at Wilmington which is First month third 1750."

The historical background of the Friends Meeting in Wilmington includes at least seven meetings which were settled prior to 1738. In

BRADFORD MEETING HOUSE

point of time New Castle seems the first since it was allowed by the Philadelphia Quarterly Meeting First month 1684. However, New-Wark (Carrcroft) was permitted by Chester Quarterly Meeting 12th month, 1685. "Agreed that the Friends in New Castle County according to their proposition may erect or set up a six weeks' meeting as they shall see cause." Gilbert Cope, the genealogist, suggests in the Newark minute book: "Instead of a six weeks meeting they appear to have established a monthly meeting and although done with the consent of Chester Quarterly Meeting, yet they did not join the Friends of Chester in their quarterly meetings until 1693."

There is no question that Newark Monthly Meeting, housed at Center, was the mother of them all for appeals were made to Newark Monthly Meeting by White Clay Creek (Stanton), Center, New Garden, Iron Hills, London Grove, Hockessin, Bradford, and Kennett all within a ten-mile radius of the Wilmington meeting which is now celebrating its 200th anniversary.

1 Scharf—History of Delaware—Philadelphia, 1888
2 Ezra Michener—A Retrospect of Early Quakerism—Philadelphia, 1860

THE SECOND MEETING HOUSE
at Fourth and West Streets

Benjamin Ferris

Transcript of the artist's comments

A View of Friends Meeting House, Wilmington, Del., 1817

The Town of Wilmington in the State of Delaware was settled and laid out as a Town about the year 1734. A Charter was granted in the year 1736 by which it was incorporated. Two years afterwards the Society of Friends built a Meeting house 25 Feet long and 26 ft. wide which is yet standing and is used as a School house. It is dated on the end Fronting High Street 1738. In ten years from that time the Society had increased so much that another Place of Worship became necessary and in the year 1748 the Building represented by above drawing was erected. It was Square each side measuring forty eight feet and would accommodate a Congregation of about 500 persons. In the year 1816 Sixty eight years from the period of its erection, the number of Families belonging to the Society of Friends who resided in the Town and its immediate vicinity was 120 composed of more than Seven hundred persons, and their Meeting house being too small a new one was commenced that year and finished the year following and on the 25th of 9th mo. 1817 first opened as a place of public Worship. In the Autumn of that Year the House above represented was taken down. The Sketch from which the above drawing was made was carefully taken by the Painter a short time before the demolition of the Building, and every object however minute was sketched. The position of the Artist at the time of taking the View was a little East of South from the corner of the Meeting house distant about One hundred and twenty feet.

RETROSPECT OF WILMINGTON FRIENDS*

William Ralph Gawthrop

WHEN in 1638 the Dutchman Peter Minuit brought two Swedish ships to anchor in a Delaware tributary, which he named Christina in honor of the infant Swedish queen and on whose rocky shore he landed to claim it as New Sweden, George Fox, the weaver's son, of Leicestershire, was but a lad of fourteen. Although, as he later wrote, he even then "knew purity and righteousness," he was yet to suffer the inner turmoil and despair that drove him to forsake father, mother and all other relations, and travel up and down "as a stranger in the earth," seeking the comfort of truth. Five weary years were to pass before he was to hear a voice say, "There is one, even Christ Jesus, who can speak to thy condition." And a hundred more would come and go, and he be forty-seven of them dead, before in Willingtown, above Christina's rocks, a handful of his followers would build a little house in which to worship God.

In the spring of 1735, Elizabeth Shipley of Ridley Township, Pennsylvania, was concerned to visit Friends in Maryland. As she made her journey southward, fording the rocky and turbulent Brandywine and then up the hill by King's Road, there is no reason to suppose she realized this was the very path George Fox had taken sixty-three years before. No more is there reason to suppose her thoughts were on the dream of a half dozen years ago, in which, riding horseback to the south, she had ascended a high hill from which she viewed a land of surpassing beauty, with green plains, wide rivers and winding streams; and to her query what place this might be her guide had answered it was the will of Providence that her husband and his family should settle here, to become instruments of great benefit to place and people alike, and with the blessing of Heaven on them and on their labors.

But, whatever her thoughts that day, it is recorded[1] that, as she reached the summit of the hill, there came to view the very scene she had beheld in her dream and now vividly recalled. There to the west the green hills descended to Mill Creek and Deer Creek. There

---

*Adapted from an address presented at the Bicentennial Celebration of the Wilmington Monthly Meetings of Friends.

wound the Christina and, scattered near it to the south, were the fifteen or twenty houses of newly founded Willingtown. And to the east the Brandywine curved into sight and, blending with the Christina, flowed lazily beyond to the broad waters of the Delaware.

But no more vivid was her remembrance of the scene than of the prophetic words that had accompanied her earlier vision. Pondering them now she was convinced it was consistent with divine will for them to remove to this new settlement.

And so she told husband William when, her Maryland visit done, she came again home. And he, though well satisfied with Ridley and how things went with them there, at length took himself to Willingtown. He found Elizabeth's judgment vindicated indeed. So much so that before he returned home he had purchased land in Willingtown. This was in May of 1735. In August he came again to Willingtown, bought more land and in the autumn, with his wife and two small children, removed to the one story brick house he had built some fifty feet west of the westerly side of Shipley Street a little below Fourth Street. It was in this house that the Shipleys, with Joseph Hewes, Thomas West (uncle of Benjamin, the painter), David Ferris (pioneer worker with John Woolman in the cause of abolition), Edward Tatnall (father of Joseph the industrialist, leading citizen and friend of Washington), and others, held the first meetings for worship in the town.[1]

The following year meetings for worship were held in William Shipley's new and larger house which Friend Griffith Marshall, bricklayer, built him on the west corner of Fourth and Shipley Streets. The meetings for worship were formally sanctioned by Chester Quarterly Meeting on twelfth month thirteenth, 1737.

In the fall of 1738, on land given by William Shipley, Friends built their first meeting house, the tiny building familiar to us all from the contemporary sketch. One wall may still be seen in the facade of the old Friends School building on West Street.

The next decade brought rapid increase to the meeting. The little house could no longer accommodate the growing society and in 1748 they built a larger one directly opposite, utilizing the old house for their school, which continues to the present and was the first of a dozen and more different schools which various Friends conducted in Wilmington through the years.[2]

Friends of New Castle and Newark were now more and more in

attendance at the Wilmington meeting. At last the older meetings yielded to the thrifty younger one. A Monthly Meeting for Friends of Wilmington and New Castle particular meetings was settled at Wilmington third month fourteenth, 1750, by order of Chester Quarterly Meeting. Newark Meeting was laid down in 1754, New Castle in 1758.[3]

With the resignation of the Quaker members of the Pennsylvania assembly Friends in Wilmington were to feel the persecution from which they had thus far happily been free. Enactment of a strict militia law brought much suffering. So a Committee for Sufferings was appointed fourth month, 1757, including Robert Lewis, Joseph Hughes, David and Zechariah Ferris, John Perry (the first clerk of our Monthly Meeting), and others. They had much to claim their attention. For refusal to enlist Friends were fined and, the fines not being paid, their property was distrained, often for twice or thrice the value of the fines, and usually in form of tools of labor, household furniture or other most essential things. In the case of William Shipley's son, William, the cradle was seized in which his child lay dying.

The stirring days of the Revolution did not leave Wilmington Friends undisturbed. The memorable part John Dickinson played in that crisis will be left for better telling by another. Nor is there time to relate the tales of lesser lights and their contribution to the history of the time. Such tales as how, when British occupied the town after their victory of the Brandywine, Friend John Stapler, a staunch adherent to royalty yet true to the rebels in this dark hour, came to the rescue of the rebel Captain Kean; who, by virtue of Friend Stapler's pillow and the borrowed garb of corpulent Friend John Benson, escaped disguised as a dropsical Quaker taking his constitutional.[4]

On eighth month twenty-eighth, 1777, the Committee for Sufferings reported: "We are given to understand that Friends Meeting House in this town is taken up with soldiers, who broke into it yesterday and that (although upon some Friends demanding it to hold meeting in today) some of them promised we should have it by 11 o'clock, yet they did not perform but kept possession and Friends held meeting under a shady tree in the grave-yard."

At this time Elizabeth Shipley, at eighty-seven, lay in her last illness. But even so she was able, through the gloom that seemed enveloping all, to evince the faith and vision that had led her to Willingtown so many years before. To friends calling on her one evening she said, "But I have seen, in the light of the Lord, that the invader of our land shall be driven back; for the arm that is mighty to save and able to deliver from the hand of the oppressor, is stretched forth for the deliverance of this nation, which, I am firm in the faith, will secure its independence." Shortly after this she was removed to London Grove where, on tenth month tenth, 1777, she died and there was buried.[1]

The epidemic of yellow fever, which first made its appearance at Philadelphia in 1793, reached Wilmington five years later. James Lea, senior, two sons of Joseph Tatnall, and others fell victims to the dread disease. The second and more devastating visitation was in 1802 and of its eighty-two victims the last was John Ferris, junior (father of Benjamin, the historian). This devoted Friend, a member of the Board of Health, in great benevolence of spirit ministered constantly to all the sick and dying. The former he made a point to visit twice daily; for the latter he, often unassisted, provided proper burial. In this service he gave his life.[1]

In 1815 a concern arose among Friends that they had outgrown the quarters which the founders had provided. The membership amply filled the house on first day mornings, religiously minded neighbors being thus discouraged from attendance and visiting ministers being handicapped by lack of accommodation for their would-be hearers.

A committee of fifteen appointed to investigate recommended construction of a larger building on the same lot. William Poole, Jacob Alrichs and Benjamin Ferris, as a sub-committee, prepared and submitted plans. The general committee, with Benjamin Ferris as clerk and John Jones as treasurer, was continued and authorized to proceed with the work. Jesse Betts was made responsible for the carpentry and Thomas Spackman for the brick and stonework.

From the carefully compiled list of one hundred and forty-five persons participating, either by cash contributions (ranging from ten to seven hundred and fifty dollars and totalling over thirteen thousand dollars) or by services of various kinds, it would appear that almost the entire membership must have had part in the enterprise.[5] Among the list were the following:

The Meeting House, Tenth and Harrison Streets, 1938

Joseph Shipley, grandson of William, and his three children, Thomas, Samuel and Sarah.

Eli and Samuel Hilles, staunch abolitionists, who conducted a large and successful girls boarding school at Tenth and King Streets. Samuel was the first head of Haverford College (1835-1838)[6] and later (1852) was President of the first Board of Education in Wilmington.[2]

Samuel Wollaston, who later conceived and developed the Brandywine Cemetery project and was the great great grandson of Thomas Wollaston, previously mentioned as perhaps the first Quaker settler in these parts.

James Wilson, the printer and publisher.

Edward, son of Joseph Tatnall, and Sarah, Edward's wife.

Evan Lewis, William Seal, Benjamin Webb and Jacob Alrichs, the first of whom had just sold to the others, as trustees of the African School Society, a lot on Sixth Street west of Tatnall, on which a school for colored children was built.

John Bullock, who from 1821 to 1826 conducted a very successful boarding school for boys at Ninth and Tatnall Streets.

William Warner, who with his father and brother founded what is now the Warner Company.

Thomas Alrichs, who, like Jacob already named, descended from Peter who came to New Castle with his uncle, Jacob, when the latter became governor in 1657.[2] (One may speculate as to whether Peter was in that first "very precious" meeting that George Fox held in New Castle.)

The new meeting house was first used for worship on ninth month twenty-fifth, 1817.

With such evidence of unity as is given by the general cooperation of the membership in the building project, it is difficult to conceive that they were soon to suffer a tragic separation. Tragic in the true sense it doubtless was, for there is reason to think that the division of 1827 was not of their making and that Friends in Wilmington, as in many other communities, would have continued on their single way but for external influences that incited to discord and strife.

However much Wilmington Friends may have been affected by

the words of Elias Hicks, to whose ministry the eventual separation
has in large part been attributed, the fact is that the new house had
scarcely been built when he paid Wilmington the first of a series of
visits that were to continue at intervals almost till his death.[7]

He came to first day meeting, both morning and afternoon on
eleventh month sixteenth, 1817, when he was in his own words
"favored with ability to preach the gospel in the demonstration of the
spirit, suited I trust, to the states of many, or most, of the people
which composed those large assemblies, and I left them with peace
of mind."

Again on seventh day, tenth month twenty-third, 1819, he attended here a large meeting by appointment, which was a "solemn
instructive season, worthy of grateful remembrance."

On first day, twelfth month third, 1826, he spoke both morning
and afternoon. From the stenographic record[8] of the sermons it is
conservatively estimated that he preached in all about two and one-
half hours.

Ninth month twentieth, 1828, he visited, at Center, the first
Monthly Meeting, composed of Preparative Meetings of Center and
Wilmington, held after the separation. The fact that, as he reports,
the house could not contain the attenders is not surprising to those
who know its size. But the following day when he attended meeting
in Wilmington, "as their meeting house was small, Friends procured
the court house in that place to hold the meeting in. The meeting
was very large, and we had a very favoured opportunity to declare
the truth among them. . . and Friends were made to rejoice for
the unmerited favor."

On his last visit to Wilmington, first day, twelfth month fourteenth
1828, he attended very large meetings both forenoon and afternoon.
"In the forenoon meeting I had good service, but in the afternoon I
was mostly silent, as the people appeared to be too much hungering
for words, and too indifferent and careless in putting in practice what
they had already heard and knew to be their duty. Hence I was led
to set them an example of silence."

Those Friends who, in 1827, withdrew from the Fourth and West
Meeting continued to hold meetings for business there for some time
afterwards. But in 1828 another meeting house was built at Ninth
and Tatnall Streets. Here Samuel Hilles was a leading figure for many

The Meeting House, Ninth and Tatnall Streets. Removed 1914

years, while his brother Eli remained at the Fourth and West Meeting. Here also, in 1832, on adjoining land donated by Samuel Canby, a new building was constructed for the school which Friends had previously carried on at Eleventh and Market Streets.

The ensuing period to the Civil War brought Wilmington Friends new problems and responsibilities, especially because of their strategic position on the "Underground Railroad."

Opposition to slavery was, of course, no new concern to them. The efforts of the first David Ferris in this cause have already been mentioned. The importation or exportation of slaves to or from the State had been forbidden by law in 1787. In the "Delaware Society for Promoting the Abolition of Slavery, for Superintending the Cultivation of Young Free Negroes, and for the Relief of those who may be unlawfully held in Bondage," organized in 1788, Friends, including William Poole, Cyrus Newlin and Edward Gilpin, took active part.[2]

But in the best known work, the Underground Railroad, in which Benjamin, William and Thomas Webb, Isaac S. Flint[9] and Samuel Hilles[6] assisted, one name "led all the rest." Thomas Garrett, who came to Wilmington in 1822, gave all his substance and the best years of his life to the service of those he called "God's poor," nearly twenty-nine hundred of whom he personally helped to freedom and only one of whom was recaptured.[9]

Emma Worrell, of beloved memory, principal of our school from 1867 to 1869, once described the first day school, which she helped to found, as "that modern force in our Society which has done more to enlarge the scope of thought, to stir the whole life of the meeting, than anything since the old days of conflicting thought and great preaching. The movement had gained some foothold in Philadelphia and West Chester before it was proposed here in 1867."[5] The originator of the scheme and the first principal was T. Clarkson Taylor, the popular and successful teacher who had come from Virginia in 1850 and, after serving as principal of Friends School, established the Taylor Academy at Eighth and Wollaston Streets.

In the time of most of us now living probably the outstanding Friends in Wilmington were William and Emma Bancroft. Their gentleness, wisdom and spiritual leadership would have set them apart without their benefactions to worthy causes without number. Swarthmore and Antioch Colleges, George School, the parks of Wilmington, the campus of our own school, all are reminders of their generosity.

1917 brought to another generation the recurrent test of Friends' principles that always comes with war. Out of the trial of the World War came at least one lasting good to Quakerism. The call to service of humanity was heard by Friends everywhere and, in the relief work of the American Friends Service Committee, Friends began again to learn what they should never have forgotten; that in the true love of Christ there are no separations or divisions.

As to other Quaker communities these lessons came to Wilmington, especially through the foreign service of Malcolm A. Brosius, George Downing, William Eves, Ruth Hoopes, Robert and Katherine Maris, Thomas H. Philips and J. Edgar Rhoads.

In the years that have followed Wilmington Friends have drawn increasingly together, as individuals and in their Friendly work of peace, education, social service and other joint concerns; in all of which both help and inspiration have come from the many who have been drawn to membership with Friends and to whom there are no kinds of Friends.

Today Friends in Wilmington are not many; no more, certainly, than in the later days of William and Elizabeth Shipley. But for our tasks—seemingly more complex yet surely no greater than theirs—we may find strength in the reminder that Christ's promise was to two or three gathered in his name; that he was but one and those with him in the upper room but twelve; that the Kingdom of God, as then, is still within, at hand.

Whatever the tasks that lie ahead, whatever of success or failure may be to come, we know this: that, if strength came to those early Friends through unity in love and spirit and purpose, we shall thus be strong.

Within the month the two Monthly Meetings of Friends in Wilmington have recorded the following minute:

"In a renewed and deepened sense of the kinship of all men as sons of God and bearers of his inner witness, we realize and cherish our unity as Friends. Mindful of our common spiritual heritage, we recognize no divisions or barriers that can separate us in the love of

Christ.   Under the power of his love we seek together still further
unity of spirit, mind and action in all ways that may serve him."

[1] Ferris, "Original Settlements on the Delaware," Wilmington, 1846.

[2] Scharf, "History of Delaware," Philadelphia, 1888.

[3] Michener, "A Retrospect of Early Quakerism," Philadelphia, 1860.

[4] Montgomery, "Reminiscences of Wilmington," Wilmington, 1846.

[5] Worrell, "The Meeting House and Some of Its People," paper delivered
   9-22-17.

[6] Hilles, "Memorials of the Hilles Family," privately printed, Cincinnati,
   1928.

[7] Journal of Elias Hicks, New York, 1832.

[8] "The Quaker," Philadelphia, 1827.

[9] Smedley, "Underground Railroad," Lancaster, 1883.

QUAKER EDUCATION IN WILMINGTON

Anna Merritt Worth and Committee

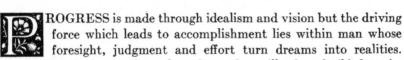ROGRESS is made through idealism and vision but the driving force which leads to accomplishment lies within man whose foresight, judgment and effort turn dreams into realities. Some point the way, others clear the paths, still others build, but the trail blazing and the building know no end. The needs of civilization are met only so long as noble men and women live and dream and love their fellow men.

Such is the history of Quaker education in Delaware. In the early records of the Wilmington Meeting are the names of Shipley, Ferris, Bringhurst, Wood, Way, Hilles, Canby, Tatnall, Stapler and many others. All these gave much of their time, energy and means to the cause of education. If they sponsored educational methods which, in the light of present knowledge, seem crude and inadequate, nevertheless by the standards of their time these leaders were truly progressive. No doubt they were even censured for their liberalism.

The early Quakers in this country must have brought many of their ideas of education from England. The English Friends had renounced Ecclesiastical traditions and had also substituted for the classical education given at Westminster, Winchester, Oxford and Cambridge one that was more practical and conducive to a well rounded character. George Fox in his "Journal" urged the establishment of a school for instructing girls and young maidens in "whatsoever things were civil and useful in the creation" and of "a school to teach languages together with the nature of herbs, roots, plants and trees." [1] Penn advised for his children "such moral training as would be consistent with truth and goodness" and "the more useful parts of mathematics as building ships, measuring, surveying, dialing, navigation". In conclusion he added: "Agriculture is especially in my eye; let my children be husbandmen and housewives. . . This leads to God and the works of God." [2]

In 1736 there were but thirty-three houses in Willingtown. Twelve years later (1748), the present Friends School was started in the small Meeting on "Quaker Hill", then outside the limits of the town. It was for the poor of the neighborhood and was to teach the rudiments of reading, writing and "ciphering". This philanthropic interest in the schooling of the poor had long been a concern of the English Quakers. William Braithewaite, an English Friend, in his book "Beginnings of Quakerism", wrote: "Each particular meeting should be expected to care for its poor, to find employment for such as want work or cannot follow their former callings by reason of the Evil therein . . . to help parents in the education of their children that there may not be a beggar amongst us."[3]

Wilmington Monthly Meeting, comprised of Wilmington and New Castle Preparative Meetings, was established in 1750. Following this date there were frequent references in the minutes to schools under the Meeting's direction. Financial support in the form of bequests soon followed. Measured by modern standards these gifts seem small, but they loomed large at a time when a day's wage was thirty-three cents and building brick two dollars sixteen cents a thousand. Only a few of the many early gifts can be mentioned here.[4]

In the minutes of the Meeting held 2nd mo. 9th, 1758, it is stated that "Wilmington Preparative Meeting acquainted this Meeting that Joshua Way had left the sum of twenty pounds currency to Wilmington particular meeting to be applied to the use of schools."

Extract from the will of Benjamin Ferris, 1778:

"Item, I will and Bequeath unto the Monthly Meeting of Friends in Wilmington, the Sum of twenty-five Pounds, to be paid by my Executrix hereinafter named, within twelve months after my decease— and the Interest arising therefrom, to be applyd yearly by said Meeting, for Schooling poor Children, either White or Black who are not under the immediate care of any Society, at the School that is under the Inspection of Friends".

Extract from the will of David Ferris, 1783:

"Item, I give & bequeath unto the Monthly Meeting of Friends in the 5th Borough, One hundred & thirty three such Pieces of Eight as afs., to be paid as herein after mentioned, & when received to be to use, and the Interest arising therefrom, to be applyd by the 5th Meeting, for the Schooling of Poor Children, White or Black, that have no right in any religious Society—"

Extract from the will of Stephen Stapler, 3rd mo. 1798:

"I do therefore now give and bequeath the sum of forty pounds to said Monthly Meeting, in trust, to be paid by my Exect- as soon as conveniently may be after my decease and to be applied agreably to said institution."

Extract from the will of John Wood, 15th of 2nd mo. 1815:

"Item, I give and bequeath to the Monthly Meeting of Friends in Wilmington aforesaid, one share of stock, in the Bank of Delaware, to be by them discretionally applied to the education of poor children."

Under the date 1794 appears a record of a gift from John Dickinson, 200 pounds "for the schooling of poor children under the care of Friends."

During this early period the more well-to-do Friends hired tutors for their children. If they were obliged to employ the itinerant teacher just off a boat and passing through the town, they did not fare so well for many such were lacking both in morals and learning. According to Benjamin Ferris, by the year 1780 "things were not quite so bad in Wilmington. The teachers were frequently good moral characters though often very deficient in other respects. The course of instruction very rarely extended beyond reading, writing and arithmetic."[5]

In Joseph Bringhurst's Journal written in 1797 are the following terse remarks:

"The world is generally speaking a Fool. It will lavish money away on superfluous trifles and draw up its purse-strings when solid advantages are to be purchased. Hence this country is overflowed with many Tutors who are blockheads and many who ought to be pupils. . . . I am daily employed in forming a System of Geography for Ziba (Ferris); for I cannot find any system that is proper to be placed in the hands of an American boy."[6]

The parents perforce supplied the religious training and set a rigid standard for their children's upbringing. One can imagine many a mother or father using Anthony Purver's poem "Counsel to Friends' Children",[7] if not as a bedtime story, at least as a daily guide and stern warning. Based on Holy Scriptures it was thorough in its instructions and frightening in its implications.

"Fear, fear the Lord, his awful Presence fear
And dare not tire for he is ever near."

"Dress not to Please nor imitate the Nice
Desire not many things nor bere much Love
Young Friends, your Portion is in Heaven above.
Here you must live a self-denying Life
And Share with us in Suffering, Scorn and Strife."

"Nor useless Sights nor Trifles then attend
But leave the Child at home and bring the Friend.
There wait to feel the Living Pow'r arise
There breathe to God your wishes and your Sighs."

"And you, their Parents, your Assistance lend
T'explain and make successful what is penned."

The founding of Friends School ushered in the era of small schools which continued until about 1830 when public schools came into being. Little has been written of these early schools or their teachers, and only a few bare facts of their existence and maintenance are recorded in the early minutes. In 1757 the following minute appears in the record of the Wilmington Monthly Meeting: "Wilmington Preparative Meeting having concluded and agreed to give up the School House to the employers of the master for the use of a school, they keeping the same in Repare at their own Expence. This Meeting doth confirm the same until further order."

At about this time each child paid two dollars and a half per quarter to the master. One suspects even this fee may have seemed exorbitant to certain parents, for in 1774 the Wilmington Monthly Meeting sent to the Quarterly Meeting an answer to a query relative to education as follows: "With Respect to the education of the youth there appears a very great deficiency, though some are careful both by precept and example to do their duty therein." And in 1777 the following minute appears:

"We the Committee appointed to visit Families of Friends amongst us as are Deficient in the Education of the Youth in the Way of Plainness of Dress, Address etc,, have agreeable thereto visited such within the Compass of our Monthly Meeting as far

FRIENDS SCHOOL AT NINTH AND TATNALL STREETS - 1913

as we felt our way open in Love to a degree of Peace in our own Minds."

> Benjamin Hough
> Caleb Seal
> Wm. Brown

> Hannah Jackson
> Jane Reynolds
> Rebekah Wood
> Dorcas Brown

The line separating the signatures of the men and women throws light on the custom of the times.

In 1779 there were several schools in Wilmington conducted by Friends. Boys and girls were apparently taught separately, the girls' schools being in the minority. Concerning these schools the following report was made:

"We the committee respecting schools having several times met do find there is one school under the direction of the preparative meeting, one other schoolmaster a member and employed by some friends with others, two school mistresses not members to which many Friends children are sent with others, there being no mistresses school under the direction of the preparative meeting which we believe is much wanted."

> Philip Jones
> Lida Ferris
> Joseph Chambers
> Joseph Warner
> Nathan Wood
> John Milnor

In this same year the first mention is made of a school fund. Cyrus Newlin was recommended as treasurer of the fund and at the same meeting an annual report was considered.

In 1791 only two schools were reported, one conducted by a man and the other by a woman. In 1792 the minutes of the Wilmington Monthly Meeting recorded that "a lot of ground had been provided by Wilmington Preparative Meeting and a School House erected". In this same year there were "three schools in the care of Friends, two belonging to Meeting, also house belonging to Friends' Meeting at White Clay Creek." This school house is still standing in Stanton. Also in the same year appears the following minute:

"That part respecting schools was read as also a minute from the Quarterly Meeting appointing a committee to attend the Monthly Meetings, most of whom attended and labored to promote the raising of a Fund agreeably to the advice of Yearly Meeting. The sentiment of divers of the members of this meeting were expressed on the subject, and it appears that friends generally write in authorization the present school committee with addition of Caleb Seal, John Elliott, Stephen Stapler and George Spackman to provide a suitable plan and solicit friends to go into a general subscription for the purpose aforesaid."

At each Monthly Meeting a school committee was appointed or the same one continued to visit the schools under its care. There was apparently some difficulty in securing good teachers in those days. Ferris gives this account: "About the year 1787 the committee having charge of the school 'on the hill' procured a teacher from Philadelphia, who was at that time accounted an extraordinary scholar, as he could teach Latin and Greek. He introduced as an additional branch of instruction, English grammar, but for want of suitable books for the purpose, his effort was an entire failure. No other branches were attempted. Geography was no more thought of as a branch of school education than Astronomy."[5]

It was in this same year, 1787, that John Webster, the principal of Friends School, was unable to control some of his pupils. There are records of the mischievous boys of the school "barring out" teacher and elders of the Meeting by blocking up all doors and windows. It was the day before Christmas and they were to be denied the holiday! Though to us this revolt may seem justified, such was not the mind of the stern elders of those early days when "to spare the rod was to spoil the child". This same John Webster, according to the old records, advised that whipping be inserted in the minutes as a necessary means of discipline. Evidently his disciplinary methods were effective, for it is said James A. Bayard, Louis McLane, Caesar Rodney and E. W. Gilpin were four of his students.[8] They became outstanding citizens, three as United States senators, and one as chief justice of the State of Delaware. Customs change, however, and in 1846, before the state school convention, Benjamin Webb was urging the repudiation of this form of punishment.[9]

In 1793 there were "three schools in the care of Friends in Wilmington and a fund established, of two hundred dollars, for the education of poor children". This is the year in which the first standing committee to look after schools is mentioned. In 1795 "a want of well qualified tutors is the subject of complaint in divers places."

In 1810 there were five schools under the direction of the Wilmington Monthly Meeting. In 1812 there was only one, but there were "several in borough taught by Friends to which some Scholars have been sent by the committee on account of the School Fund". In 1813 there were ten schools "within the verge of this meeting" supported to some extent by funds for the use of poor children, though only one of these schools was under the direction of the school committee.

In 1819 the following school committee was appointed:

Isaac Jackson   William Lea   Evan Lewis
Ziba Ferris   Samuel Hilles

In 1824 for the first time there was a report from the Women's Meeting that there were two schools under their care which were visited regularly. In 1829 the minutes recorded the concern that the pupils were not being brought to mid-week Divine Worship, primarily because the teachers were not all members of the Meeting. The committee proposed that "in conformity with the advice from our Yearly Meeting the school hereafter may be taught by our members of whom it will be expected that they shall exert a proper care to bring the children to our religious meetings on week-days".

The early eighteen hundreds ushered in a new era of educational opportunity in Wilmington, that of the private Boarding School. These schools drew their patronage not only from the surrounding States but from distant points as well. Friends were leaders in this field as well as in the various day schools and the schools for the poor. It must be remembered that there were still no public schools.

Eli and Samuel Hilles, brothers, conducted a flourishing school for girls in a large double house they erected at the corner of Tenth and King Streets (the site now occupied by the Municipal Building) which apparently was the only school of its kind at that period in the United States, for "females" came not only from many States but even from the West Indies. French was taught to those who desired it and "a little of the ornamental of drawing". Mrs. Susan Hilles Sherman in her sketch of the Hilles properties published in 1914 wrote: "It is not unusual for a stranger to call and ask to see the house and garden, saying, 'I have often been told about it by my mother'."[10] According to Powell[11] Eli Hilles withdrew in 1828 and four years later Samuel Hilles was called to the newly founded Haverford College. The Hilles School continued, however, for many years under new management.

John Bullock, also a member of the Society of Friends, opened a successful boarding school for boys in 1821, first on King Street but later removed to Ninth and Tatnall Streets. This was in existence for twenty-five years and was well attended, many coming from distant sections of the country. After Bullock's death in 1847, Samuel Alsop, a mathematician, carried on the school, assisted by Theodore Hyatt who later bought the school and turned it into a Military Academy.

Samuel Smith in 1829 started a boarding school for boys between Third and Fourth on West Street. This school maintained a high grade of excellence, having fine apparatus and equipment throughout. Many subjects were taught including Greek, Latin and higher mathematics. To quote from an advertisement of the time: "The terms of admission (including boarding, washing and instruction) are, for the Mathematical and English Department 150 dollars per annum, payable quarterly in advance, and six dollars per quarter are added for each language in which any pupil may receive instruction." Samuel Smith was a fine teacher and a most lovable character. We are told the boys would gather about him after classes and enjoy his careful explanations of difficult problems. Among those interested in the school were William Gibbons, M. D., Eli Hilles, Benjamin Ferris and Ziba Ferris. In 1839 Samuel Smith left Wilmington and the school was discontinued.

T. Clarkson Taylor opened a boys' school in 1857 at Eighth and Wollaston Streets. Immediately before this, from 1852 to 1857, he was principal of Friends School and was most successful in bringing that school up to a higher standard than it had enjoyed at any previous period. In five years the attendance had so increased that, the Meeting funds being too low to permit of enlarging the building, Clarkson Taylor decided to start a school of his own. The Friends cooperated in this and approved of allowing as many of the Friends' children as so desired to enter the new institution. It was called the T. Clarkson

Taylor's Scientific and Commercial Academy but later, when Milton Jackson became associated with the school, the name was changed to The Taylor and Jackson Academy. It was a large, three-storied brick building on what was then the outskirts of the town. Boys from ten years of age upwards were there given a thorough and useful education. Many boys went from there to college or into business. After Clarkson Taylor's death in 1871, his brother Jonathan carried on the school for a few years and in 1875 the Board of Education bought the building for a public school. Clarkson Taylor was not only a great influence for good in the field of education but he is to be remembered for his spiritual guidance as well. He was the first "recommended minister" and his active work in school did not prevent his giving much of his time to the Meeting.

Emma Worrell taught for a short time in the Taylor and Jackson Academy but previously conducted a "modest school" for girls at 809 Tatnall Street. In 1867 she was called as principal to Friends School where she remained for about three years. In 1873 she resumed her own school on Tatnall Street, moving in 1879 to 811 Washington Street. Her enrollment numbered from twenty to forty, many coming from a distance and boarding at private homes during the term. She was held in warm affection by her students and up to the time of her death in her ninety-seventh year she received many visitors from among the alumni. Even in her advanced age Emma Worrell's mind was alert and her sympathies warm. In the new Friends School on Alapocas Drive, her portrait hangs in the library which bears her name.

Soon after the division of the Society of Friends in 1827, the Orthodox Friends established their own school. On 7th mo. 27th, 1831 a committee composed of Margaret Morton, Martha Stroud, Mary Richardson, Rachel Bullock, Elizabeth Canby, Mary C. Tatum and M. H. Hilles reported "that since our last Monthly Meeting a school for small children has been established under the care of Margaretta Hughes." This school was located at Eleventh and Market Streets. The minutes of the Women's Meeting held 8th mo. 27th, 1832 state that: "A bequest has been made to the Monthly Meeting by our honored Friend Samuel Canby . . . of a lot of ground and the sum of One Thousand Dollars to be applied to the benefit of a school under care of the Meeting . . ." On 5th mo. 4th, 1833 the new school was nearly ready. The little one-room frame schoolhouse was built on a lot in the middle of the block bounded by Tenth, Orange, Ninth

FRIENDS SCHOOL, FOURTH AND WEST STREETS, 1937

and Tatnall Streets. On the adjoining lot stood the Meeting House.
In 1874, a second room of brick construction was added at a cost of
$1949.27.

The teaching staff was composed of one to three teachers. The
school reached its peak of popularity during the Civil War period,
when fifty-five scholars were registered, nineteen of them being members of the Meeting. In 1871 the enrollment had dropped to ten, and
the school committee made a "change in management of the school
by substituting the payment of a salary to the teacher instead of the
previous method. The impression appears to have been given that
it was intended to make it (the school) strictly select, which they
believe, will account in good measure for the smallness of the school.
It is hoped this will not be of long continuance." Under the new
regime the school revived and until the turn of the century averaged
about twenty-five children. After 1890, but few children of Friends
attended the school. The older children were attracted to Westtown
and other private schools and by 1904 the Meeting school appears to
have been largely a school for small children, including those of kindergarten age. In 1909, the school passed from the care of the Meeting,
but was evidently used for a private school until the property was
sold in 1913.

The names of only a few of the teachers appear in the Meeting
minutes. Familiar names, however, are those of Rebecca D. Maris
(1874), Mary C. Bundy (1882), Joseph Rhoads, Jr. and his wife
Harriet M. Rhoads (1885), Mary H. Tatnall (1887), Mary A. Pierson
(1888), Myra T. Embree (1901) and Jean Harris who was the last
teacher appointed by the Meeting.

Life in the little school at Ninth and Tatnall Streets was very
pleasant. Some now living remember it well. Just within the entrance
gate on Tatnall Street was a faucet with drinking cup. A board walk
led to the schoolhouse, shaded by great maples. In the rectangle
made by fences, meeting house and school house, stood the finest oak
in Wilmington, spreading its branches over an immense area and in
the angles of whose great roots small children built houses of sticks
and moss. There was a wide range of ages with Katy Pyle, a tall girl
in her teens, at one end and at the other a little fellow in a Scotch
kilt, the only boy who had not attained to trousers. During the long
noon recess, after lunches were eaten from gay red, white and blue
boxes featuring the presidential candidates, Hayes and Tilden, such

games as fox-and-geese or hide-and-seek were the favorites. Lessons made little impression on the younger children though there were general exercises in which the whole school recited in concert the multiplication table and the capitals of all the countries in the world.

The rapid growth of private and public schools in Wilmington and vicinity appears to have affected enrollment in those schools under the care of the Monthly Meetings. In answer "to the Interrogatories of the yearly meetings committee on the subject of Schools" 8th mo. 2nd, 1833, the Wilmington Monthly Meeting reported about one hundred ten children under its care, but only two schools under its direction, one in Wilmington, probably at Fourth and West Streets, the other at Brandywine Village. "Both of these schools are for females except that a few small boys are occasionally admitted." Twenty-eight children of Friends attended private schools, "respectably conducted" in most cases by Friends, while but thirteen of the forty-five children in Meeting-sponsored schools were members of the Meeting. "Spelling, reading, writing and arithmetick are taught in all these schools, in several of them English grammar, geography, the use of maps and globes, History, the elements of Botany and in one of them the French language. The reading books used are the Scriptures, Murray's School Books, Young's Night Thoughts, Cowper's Task, American First Class Book, Sequel to early Lessons, etc." At this time five members of the Wilmington Meeting were attending school at Westtown.

On 12th mo. 24th, 1841, the schoolhouse at Brandywine was reported unoccupied. The committee "proposed fitting it up as dwelling house". There appears to be no further mention in the minutes of the Brandywine school.

On 4th mo. 26th, 1846, the Women's Meeting expressed a concern "which has occupied their attention for sometime, to establish a school for Females of more advanced age than the one now under their care and were desirous of our, (the Monthly Meeting's) cooperation". Cooperation was granted. The old building was demolished and a committee composed of Samuel Buzby, Ziba Ferris, Joseph Bringhurst, Joseph Bancroft, Charles Canby and Eli Hilles on 10th mo. 23rd, 1846, reported the new building nearly finished at an expense of $556.25. The exact location of this building enterprise is not known.

During this same year, 1846, Benjamin Ferris wrote of the school at Fourth and West Streets: "That house (the original Meeting House) is yet standing, with the date of its erection marked by black glazed bricks in the gable wall. It is situate on West Street, being occupied as a school house. To this useful purpose it has been devoted since the year 1748, and thousands of children have there received the first rudiments of an English education. It is built of brick, 24 feet square, and one story high. It originally had a broad penthouse, or projecting roof, at the southwest end, extending across the whole of that front."

For nearly one hundred years the minutes of the Wilmington Meeting record only two minor changes in the original structure, nor are records available to show when the physical form of the building began its change. By 1883 it had expanded to a two-story shingle roof building covering a plot thirty by sixty feet.[12] On 3rd mo. 16th, 1882 "a desire seemed to be with the committee to do our part towards placing the school on as high a plane as possible."[13] The following year $14,000 was expended on a building program, to be followed by another extension in 1889, costing $9500. Still other changes were made in the 1890's, but so far as recorded, no old building was displaced to make place for the new. The patchwork design of the present Fourth and West building facade is evidence of this gradual growth.

With the physical change of the school, came also educational progress. The problem of finding suitable teachers led to action by the Women's Meeting: 8th mo. 28th, 1846, "Mary Betts, Elizabeth Peart, Martha Hilles, Eliza Ferris and Sarah Bringhurst are appt. to have charge of both schools under the care of this mo. m. The meeting now directs that the sum of money which was collected for enabling young women to qualify themselves for teachers be placed in the hands of the sch. com. to be used at their discretion." This action was in accordance with "Christian Advices" issued by the Yearly Meeting as early as 1808:[14] "As the want of suitably qualified persons amongst Friends for teachers of schools is the occasion of serious disadvantages to the society in many places . . . we desire Friends would attend to this important point in their monthly meetings, and assist young men and women of low circumstances whose capacities and conduct may be suitable for that occupation, with the means requisite to obtain the proper qualifications; and when so qualified, afford them the necessary encouragement for their support."

For the twenty-five years following 1846, there are few written records, but the darkness is brightened by tradition which tells of the outstanding qualities of two much loved teachers, T. Clarkson Taylor and Emma Worrell. In the 1870's there were about one hundred children in the Primary, Large Girls and Boys departments. The principal and two assistants composed the teaching staff. The tuition charge was collected by the principal who in turn paid the assistants a fixed salary, the balance being his own compensation. In 1877 the principal's share was but $450.00 and the school committee ruled that the following year "the paid tuitions of all three schools shall not be less than 1000 dollars per year". It was customary that all books and teaching equipment furnished by the School Committee or the Meeting should become the property of the principal.

During 5th mo. 1876, the school committee consisting of Lucy Smyth, Thomas Worrell, Edward Garrett, Priscilla Speakman and Mary B. Pyle "decided to furnish the large north room upstairs for a boys' school to be under the charge of George Thompson who was to teach in connection with Ann Fothergill, the boys and girls reciting their lessons together in classes".

The following minute in the school committee report 9th mo. 15th, 1881, marks the beginning of a decade and a half of rapid change: "It was decided to secure the service of Isaac T. Johnson as Principal." Under his wise direction registration increased three-fold and his staff, from two assistants in 1881 to sixteen in 1895. Greek, German, History, English Literature, Science, Higher Mathematics, Elocution, were among subjects added to the curriculum. The first mention of kindergarten appears in the following curious form in the school committee minutes 5th mo. 8th, 1886: "The questions of kindergarten and one session were not considered on account of want of time." (Signed, M. B. Pyle). This indicates a hope soon to be realized. Kindergarten was started in 1889 though not mentioned in the school catalogue before 1892. By 1895 it enrolled twenty children, some of them three and one-half years of age. In addition, the school sponsored a well organized training school for kindergarten teachers.

These innovations appealed to those who wished the best in education, but such cannot be provided without cost. By the end of the century tuitions ranged from $50.00 in the Primary School, through the Intermediate School, to $150.00 for college preparation in the High School.

Men and women of mature years well remember school days of the 1890's when "each student is expected always to be polite and respectful to teachers and fellow-students. The courtesies of the home are to be practiced in all relations of school life."[15] Of these days Henry Seidel Canby has written for us a vivid description printed elsewhere in this book. Even during the period of which Canby writes important changes in curriculum were under consideration. Competition from the rapidly improving public schools played an important part in bringing definite action on these contemplated changes, but the vision and wisdom of the teaching staff and school board must be credited with the success with which steady progress has been made without loss of fundamental values.

Manual training was introduced in 1898. Since that time have been added Household Arts, "Vocal Culture", Music in its many phases, Dramatics and Art. Important as are these branches of learning, of more significance is the change in method of presentation. Acquirement of knowledge and its practical application appear to be skillfully combined in the modern project method of teaching. For most children the task of learning is now a pleasant experience. In the language of today: "Education is learning to participate in contemporary life."

Side by side with the mental development of the student, Friends School has had concern for the physical well-being of its members. The first gymnasium was provided in 1889 in the basement of the main building. It is pictured in the school catalogues of the 1890's. In 1907, the large gymnasium now standing at the Fifth Street end of the old school property was constructed and equipped at a cost of $26,917.38,[16] largely from funds provided by William P. Bancroft. This benefactor, over a period of years, so generously contributed with wise counsel and financial assistance to the welfare of Friends School, that he will remain linked traditionally with its history.

Since 1889 increasing emphasis has been laid on the value of group sports for boys and girls alike. Frequent references are found in the minutes to special funds for athletic fields and equipment. More recently the services of a school physician have been available and a qualified nurse makes daily health inspections.

These many changes, which seem largely to have had their ultimate origin in the era of Isaac Johnson, have been brought to

Photo by Sanborn Studio

FRIENDS SCHOOL, 1938

reality mostly under his successors, Herschel A. Norris, 1899-1923, Charles W. Bush, 1923-1935, and Wilmot R. Jones, 1935-.

The present aims of the school are stated thus in the educational philosophy formulated by the faculty:

"Friends School in Wilmington seeks to create for its pupils, and to help them to create for each other, a happy community in which to work and play. By means of a flexible curriculum the School aims at teaching the child to live a well-adjusted life, so that he can carry out intelligently his own worthwhile interests.

"Learning is considered rather from the viewpoint of experiencing than from that of the mere acquisition of subject-matter. The teachers consider fundamental physical and mental skills as of great importance; hence pupils are taught to meet the responsibility of laying a secure foundation in them. They are taught, furthermore, to judge open-mindedly, with respect for the ideas of others; to use time wisely; to make intelligent decisions. Opportunity is given for creative expression of all kinds, especially in the arts.

"The School is progressive to the extent that it is willing always to consider without prejudice and to adopt new theories which seem likely to contribute to the attainment of its educational objectives; these objectives are themselves open to constant modification and restatement, where the need for such modification is reasonably clear. But it is conservative in avoiding what appear to be extremes and in adhering to some of the old principles which still seem to be valid. Freedom is strongly advocated, so long as it does not stand in the way of the development of the pupil or his associates. The School seeks to place a real premium upon the acquisition of such simple social virtues as courtesy, kindliness, tolerance, and serenity of spirit."

In a physical way also the twentieth century has brought momentous changes to the school. The last addition to the old buildings came in 1912 with construction of the elementary wing, on the Fourth Street end, at a cost of $32,000.

In 1927 a serious study was first made of the possibility of a new location and new buildings for the school. A special committee surveyed the physical needs of the school, the availability of a new site and possibilities for disposing of the Fourth and West Streets property. Emma C. Bancroft in 1928 offered fifteen acres of land at Alapocas, providing a school be built within ten years. But before financial plans were fully formulated general economic conditions necessitated postponement of the project.

The matter was reopened in the summer of 1935 by an anonymous gift of $175,000 conditioned on raising an additional sum sufficient to erect new buildings. In the early winter of that year nearly one thousand friends of the school united in gifts totaling over $100,000 and the enterprise was assured. A special gift from the daughters of Emma C. Bancroft made an additional five acres of land available. Ground was broken June 4, 1936, and the new school buildings at Alapocas were formally opened September 17, 1937. Excluding land, the total cost of the project was about $345,000.

The report of the Board of Managers of the school to the Monthly Meetings, dated November 16, 1937, concluded thus:

"Now that our physical equipment approaches so near the ideal, we are sensible as never before that the reason for our School goes far beyond what buildings, however fine, can give; that now, more than ever, we must succeed in apprehending for ourselves and transmuting into the lives of our students those values of personality and living which must characterize a real Friends School."

[1] George Fox—"Journal."
[2] Penn—"Advice to His Children"
[3] William Braithwaite—"Beginnings of Quakerism."
[4] From "Accounts of the Treasurer of the Fund of Friends School."
[5] Benjamin Ferris—"A History of the Original Settlements on the Delaware."
[6] Joseph Bringhurst—in unpublished Journal
[7] Anthony Purver—"Counsel to Friends' Children."
[8] The Morning News, Wilmington, June 22, (1894)
[9] Wilmington Gazette, Sept. 4, 1846.
[10] Susan Hilles Sherman—"Sketch of the Hilles Properties, 1914."
[11] Lyman P. Powell—"The History of Education in Delaware (1893)"
[12] Catalog, Friends' School, 1894-1895.
[13] School Committee Minutes.
[14] Christian Advices—published by Yearly Meeting of Friends (1808).
[15] Friends School Catalog (1891).
[16] Private Papers of William P. Bancroft.

FRIENDS SCHOOL AS I KNEW IT
IN THE NINETIES*

Henry Seidel Canby

UR school building was symbolic of the town and the age. Across West Street was the meeting-house under its elms, solid, decorous, proportioned, meaningful. That decorum may have been outgrown, that proportion of living become impossible, yet beauty was realized there, and with beauty life. But our school was piled up, wall on wall, and roof on roof, tinned, pebbled, slated according to age, finished off with mansards in the style of the seventies and tipped by an irreverent peak or two in the taste of the nineties. It was haphazard, makeshift, ill-ordered, yet regimented internally into a fairly efficient factory where pupils could march from study room to assembly hall without much lost motion. The floors were bare, the desks uncomfortable, the walls strips of blackboard or plaster adorned with an occasional "classic" picture which no one ever thought to explain. Everything was sensible, practical, and efficient except the purpose of it all which was supposed to be education but was actually cramming under discipline. Bells rang, tickets were sold for a hygienic lunch (cream puff and cocoa), classes proceeded so effectively that no one who wished to enter college ever failed to do so, order was kept, the principal sat like a spider in his office or tiptoed like a daddy-long-legs peering through doors, all of which were glass-topped for his convenience. The Ford production line does not function more perfectly than did that school, except in education.

Inside everything was departmentalized. There was science—which had nothing to do with religion, and religion (on Fifth Day meeting and for five minutes each morning) which had nothing to do with school, and literature which was concerned with Shakespeare and the Lake Poets, and Latin which had nothing to do with anything except syntax. There were no values (with one exception) except the values of discipline and knowledge, and a sense (which I do not under-estimate) of the past. As in all American institutions of that day, foreign languages were taught for reading only, it being incredible that anyone should have to speak German or French. But the relation

(65)

*Adapted from the chapter on Education in the author's "Age of Confidence." Ferris and Rinehart, New York.

between science and our mores, or between the mechanism of physics and the mysticism of Fifth Day meeting, or between history and the very bad politics in action at the city hall only five blocks away, or between literature and the emotional content of our rather pallid lives—nothing.

But our school had its own peculiar ethics. We were a remnant of the great Quaker movement which spread from Pennsylvania north, south, west, until its shallowing waters became only an undercurrent of the communities where they still flowed. Our ethics were infused always with the central Quaker principle, that men and women being essentially good, evil was due to some obfuscation of the Inner Light through accident, or evil influence, or worldly pride. We youngsters were gathered for education from all the local sects, but whatever our home environment we could not escape the insidious Quaker idea that the world was by nature friendly, and the universe also, that there was good will in every man, that reforms did not come through laws and restrictions but by appeal to the innate goodness in every human heart. Contradictions lay all about us in a town that drank, cheated, tyrannized, and was mean, and we had, of course, some realization of this before actual experience. It was saddening as one grew older to encounter unmistakable depravity; it was puzzling to see good men conniving in dead religions or greedy commercialism, because our ethical education (like all our education) had ignored the relationships between theory and practice, or, for that matter, between theory and theory; it stunned us to discover whole ranges of emotion that the Quakers overlooked because they were not interested or because they knew that bricks to build ideal societies crumbled if the kiln fires were too hot.

Nevertheless, one was better prepared than seemed possible. The Quakers were well aware of the forces of worldliness. Under their gentle but powerful influence we acquired an instinct which subtly pervaded our later thinking. We found it difficult not to believe in the permanent possibility of good in any man. The naive (and yet not so naive either) faith in the possibilities of human nature, which was and is characteristic of many American communities, has been usually credited to our national experience in the unlimited richness of an unexploited country. A realistic study of the frontier makes this explanation often doubtful, and sometimes ridiculous. The mild but pervasive influence of the Quakers is a more probable cause, although that influence was so widespread when America was in the making that by its very dilution and absorption it lost the name of Quaker. Certainly we felt it strongly in our school and our town, and to it must be charged some of our confidence in the world.

FRIENDS IN PHILANTHROPY

Robert H. Maris

N THE Epistle of James, half a chapter is devoted to the subject of the importance of a right relationship between faith and works. In spite of times of failure, the endeavor to maintain this relationship has been characteristic of the Society of Friends throughout its history. If, as Friends claim, religion and life are inseparable, then any Christian service undertaken whether by individual or group must be the expression of an inward experience, an obedience to a hidden prompting, the following of a divine light within the soul.

It is our purpose to review briefly some of the ways in which the religious faith of Friends in Wilmington has found outward expression during the past two hundred years, particularly through connections with charitable and philanthropic organizations. The list of such organizations is long and, considering the comparatively small number of Friends in the city, they are widely represented on the boards of management of many social agencies. Mention will be made of a few enterprises for social betterment which Friends either founded or in which they have been particularly active.

First of all, perhaps, should be noted the collection of funds and the appointment of administrative committees in the Meeting itself to care for its own members as necessity required. Such care has marked the Society of Friends since its earliest days, a responsibility which grew naturally out of a tender concern for one another in times of suffering and distress. During the years, through bequests of deceased Friends, trust funds have provided some means of helping persons in need and also some assistance toward the education of children.

In 1800 there came into being what is probably the oldest charitable institution in Delaware, an organization of young women Friends which still continues under the name of the Female Benevolent Society. Perhaps no better description of it can be given than is found in Episode IV of the Pageant* which was based on an historical sketch of this society, written in 1872.

---

*See page 119   (69)

It is noteworthy that as first organized the object of the Society was not only for the relief but for the employment of the poor. "Committees shall be appointed to seek and visit, without distinction of nation or color, such persons as may be proper objects of their attention and care. These committees shall endeavor to encourage and promote industry by furnishing employment to such as might be able to work."

In the early days flax was purchased, hackled and prepared for spinning—then weighed and distributed to the spinners. When returned by them it had to be "sorted, counted and valued by the Committee," then paid for in produce. Another committee collected subscriptions to carry on the work. The community evidently appreciated the work of the Society for it received various bequests: a number of young men provided a store for their accommodation; the first year the Board of Health gave them six cords of wood to distribute, the next season it sent them $50.00; Dr. John Vaughn offered his professional services gratuitously to visit the sick and later offered to inoculate for smallpox all poor children recommended to his care. The Association for many years appears to have had no more definite title than "Female Society." A bequest from Jacob Broom to the "Female Benevolent Society" induced the members to procure an act of incorporation and to adopt the name thus given them. Jacob Broom, though not a Friend, annexed to his bequest the condition that the Association should remain "under the care of those belonging to the Society of Friends and those professing with them." The Society now carries out through other social agencies the purposes of its founders.

John Ferris, a member of a well known Quaker family, died in 1882 and by his will left directions and provision for the establishment of an institution to care for boys of delinquent conduct. Three years later the Ferris Reform School was opened on a farm a few miles west of the city. The institution, now named the Ferris Industrial School, has become a state agency, receives a state appropriation and is managed by a board of trustees appointed by the governor. To it are committed both white and colored boys, whose misdemeanors have brought them before the juvenile court.

It may be fitting to mention at this point the interest certain Friends have shown in the subject of prison reform. Efforts to secure more humane and intelligent treatment of prisoners and to abolish barbarous forms of punishment, such as the pillory and whipping post and the infliction of the death penalty, have long engaged the attention of local Friends. In recent years they have shared in the work of the Prisoners' Aid Society, an organization to investigate the needs of prisoners, to render such services as seem right and to assist the families of men serving sentences. In work of this nature Friends have appealed to the reason and conscience of their contemporaries in an effort to show that a different spirit is needed than the desire for revenge which seems to motivate much of the treatment accorded to persons convicted of crime.

The part taken by the late William P. Bancroft in projects for the benefit and enjoyment of the community deserves fuller treatment than can here be given. We make brief mention of three of his major interests for which he will long be remembered. Public parks were a chief concern of William Bancroft. Through his leadership the Board of Park Commissioners was created in 1883 and until his death in 1928 he was a member, serving as president for the fourteen years prior to 1922. Alert and farsighted as to future needs for parks, he was instrumental in securing valuable sites, many of which were his own gift to the city. The enlargement and improvement of the entire park system was a matter to which he gave much time and thought.

Another way in which William Bancroft's spirit found expression was through the Woodlawn Company, organized in 1901 for the purpose of carrying out various philanthropic activities. One of these was a large housing project in the western part of Wilmington, which was accomplished between 1903 and 1913. Twenty rows of small houses were erected, accommodating nearly four hundred families. Two objects were attained by this building operation, one being the houses themselves which provided comfortable living quarters for people of small means, the other being the income from the rent of the houses which was applied to other public benefactions. In 1919 the Woodlawn Company became Woodlawn Trustees, Inc., the profits of which were to be used entirely "for the benefit of the people of Wilmington and its vicinity." Many charitable and educational institutions have benefitted thereby, land for parks and playgrounds has been acquired and given to the city and residential districts have been planned and developed. A large tract of farming land and rough, untillable woodland north of the city extending to the state line is being held by the corporation with the thought of future development for the good of the community.

For many years William Bancroft took a leading part in a movement to make The Wilmington Institute, at that time a subscription library, free to all the inhabitants of the city. Through his efforts the state legislature passed an act in 1893 amending the charter of The Wilmington Institute whereby the city was obliged to contribute towards its support. Before that time the library had belonged to its stockholders and annual payments were required for the use of books. William Bancroft was successful in inducing a large majority of the stockholders to turn in their stock certificates to be held in trust by the Security Trust Company which still uses them in voting for members of the Board of Managers. William Bancroft remained a member of the Board until 1910.

From time to time the Society of Friends produces persons of unusual moral sensitiveness. This quality often leads to espousing the causes of individuals or groups for whom conventional society feels little if any responsibility. Such a group may be the inmates of penitentiaries, already alluded to or frequently the negro element in a community. A few words therefore should be said regarding some forms of action which Quaker concern for better inter-racial understanding has initiated n Wilmington.

The Thomas Garrett kindergarten for colored children has long been the concern of Helen S. Garrett, a granddaughter of Thomas Garrett, an outstanding Friend of the past century whose valiant service in connection with the Underground Railroad is described elsewhere in this book. Helen Garrett started the kindergarten in 1894 and has always made herself responsible for its maintenance. Since 1924 it has been housed in the colored settlement at Sixth and Walnut Streets, although the kindergarten is neither financed nor managed by that organization. The Meeting has maintained an interest in the Thomas Garrett kindergarten and has aided it financially, while the children of the First-day School have also kept in friendly touch with it.

Leaders in recent years in the movement to bring about better interracial relationships were George A. Rhoads and his wife, Frances Tatum Rhoads. These Friends were active in the formation of the Delaware Interracial Committee and two important results of a very practical nature soon developed.

First was the founding of the Industrial School for Colored Girls near Marshallton, Delaware. George Rhoads was treasurer for the committee that started the school in 1920. Later, with the aid of William P. Bancroft and Henry J. Krebs, he was able to secure a ninety-acre farm opposite the original site and in 1921 the legislature took over the school as a state institution. George Rhoads was chairman of the Board for about seven years. Withdrawing from that office on account of ill health, he continued as a member of the Advisory Board until his death in 1937.

In 1925 the Citizens Housing Corporation was organized with George Rhoads as president. The object of this enterprise was to provide better homes for Negroes at a fair rental. A survey of conditions showed that many Negroes were living in houses unfit for human habitation, in many cases being charged excessively high rent. Stock was offered at $10.00 per share and in this way houses were bought and when necessary put in good condition and leased to Negroes at a fair rate. A report of the Corporation published a few years ago states that large financial returns on an investment of this kind cannot be promised but stockholders may have the satisfaction of knowing that they are helping a much needed work in the community and that they are giving self-respecting citizens an opportunity to secure comfortable homes at reasonable cost.

The establishment of the American Friends Service Committee in April, 1917, when the United States joined the Allies in the World War gave an opportunity to Friends all over America to put their peace principles into practice. A number of young Wilmington Quakers served abroad in relief and reconstruction work in France and Poland and in the child feeding work in Germany. Many Friends took an active part in the work at home and interest still continues. In 1925 an older Friend from Wilmington, Lloyd Balderston, was sent by the A. F. S. C. on a mission to China. This experience of widely shared service has had the effect of bringing long divided groups of Friends into a realization of their basic unity.

This record of the place Friends have taken in concerns for social betterment is necessarily incomplete. Much more could be written on the subject but the instances given may make clear the connection between faith and works. We can devoutly hope that in the future this balance may still keep true and that though it may take different forms, the divine seed in the soul of man may continue to expand and bear much fruit.

THOMAS GARRETT
Quaker Abolitionist*

Thomas E. Drake

THOMAS GARRETT, 1783-1871

N THE early days of railroad building, before the Civil War, when short lines united the towns and cities of the eastern seaboard, and Baltimore and Philadelphia were pushing tracks over the mountains in a race for the rich trade of the West, the system known as the Underground Railroad received its name. Its network, begun long before its mechanical namesake came into being, spread over half of the United States, running northward through Pennsylvania, Ohio, Indiana and adjacent States, to the Canadian border. Thousands of passengers were carried on its trains in cars which ran in only one direction, from slavery to freedom. More than twenty-seven hundred of these passengers traveled through Wilmington on the famous road. Probably no other place in the whole network handled so much business as did the Wilmington station, namely the Garrett house at 227 Shipley Street. Thomas Garrett, the keeper of the station, is remembered as one of Wilmington's most renowned citizens, the equal of her great political figures such as John Dickinson, and of her great industrialists of more recent days.

Thomas Garrett's career was unusually romantic, for there is a glamour about the Underground Railroad which makes political and economic achievement seem prosaic by contrast. A generation of small boys after the Civil War thrilled to the stories of night rides, daring rescues, and brilliant escapes which were recounted by the aging participants in the Underground Railroad. The "Reminiscences" of Levi Coffin, the famous Quaker "conductor" of Indiana, were most

---

*Address presented at the Bicentennial Celebration of the Wilmington Monthly Meeting of Friends.

exciting, and stories of the Underground are still repeated in fictional biographies such as Hildegard Hoyt Swift's "Railroad to Freedom," a recent account of the life of the Negro slave-runner, Harriet Tubman. A juvenile reader of the Wilmington Public Library's well-worn copy of this book penciled the enthusiastic comment on the title page, "Swell!" The modern generation still thrills to Underground Railroad adventures.

The name itself has given rise to fantastic ideas regarding the character of the road. An Indiana school teacher gravely told a friend of mine that she had actually seen the entrance of the tunnel through which fugitives were shipped to Canada. Apparently her imagination had been so stimulated by the sight of the caves on the Indiana shore of the Ohio River, caves in which slaves were hidden after they had escaped across the river from Kentucky, that she pictured to herself a real tunnel extending all the way from southern Indiana to the Lake Erie shore. A skiff on the Ohio and a boat on Lake Erie were all that were needed to make the journey. The middle portion of the trip was provided for by Quaker engineers and conductors, racing their passengers through underground darkness while slavehunters fruitlessly sought them on the surface.

The true story of the Underground Railroad is almost as bizarre as this amusing fantasy. It was an exciting business, with secret rooms in sober Quaker houses, secret compartments in ordinary looking wagons, and frequent resort to disguises such as the gowns and bonnets of Quaker ladies which many Quaker conductors are reputed to have used for their black passengers in time of need. The pity of it is that most of the record of this exciting crusade—for a crusade it was, against the wickedness of slavery—has been lost to history. The work was done stealthily by day and quietly by night, with danger of capture for the slave and punishment for the helper always in mind. Action was more useful than words, and written words might betray the unwise writer. Some men, Thomas Garrett among them, dared to write letters when letters were required, but most of this correspondence was destroyed when it had served its immediate purpose. The true story of the Underground Railroad perished with the death of the train crews and cargo.

Knowing this to be the case, when the request came to me to speak here tonight on Thomas Garrett I accepted with the hope that I might discover a cache of documents which would add something to the familiar story of Thomas Garrett's Underground Railroad career. The standard account is in Professor Wilbur H. Siebert's great work on the Underground Railroad, published forty years ago.[1] Siebert's account is, however, little more than a condensation of the story of Thomas Garrett as told by his colored friend and co-worker, William Still. Still was the chief Underground Railroad agent in Philadelphia in the late 'forties and 'fifties. As secretary of the local "Vigilance Committee" of abolitionists he worked closely with Thomas Garrett, receiving many of the fugitive slaves whom Garrett sent north from Wilmington. Still published in 1883 an extensive account of the Underground Railroad, including a sketch of Thomas Garrett's life and some fragments of his correspondence.[2] But these fragments and this short account tell of only a few of the hundreds of shipments which Thomas Garrett made on the invisible railroad. Somewhere, I hoped, there might be documents which would open up whole new chapters in Thomas Garrett's career.

In the search for the buried treasure of letters or diaries, I have been most kindly assisted by many Wilmington people. Newspaper files, Public Library and Historical Society archives, and Federal Court records have graciously been made available to me. In addition, Miss Helen S. Garrett, granddaughter of Thomas Garrett, has allowed me to consult a most interesting scrapbook of material concerning her grandfather. Mr. John M. Mendinhall, who is also related to Thomas Garrett, has been most kind and helpful.

In seeking new light on Thomas Garrett it seemed possible that there might be correspondence preserved at the Underground Railroad stations immediately north and south of Wilmington. The Mendenhalls, Isaac and Dinah, who lived on a farm near Hamorton, Pennsylvania, were keepers of the next station northward, but inquiry discloses that whatever papers may have been kept by them were destroyed in a fire some years ago. The agent to the south, John Hunn, a Friend who lived near Middletown, Delaware, caused his personal papers to be burned before his death.[3] Written records of Thomas Garrett's Underground Railroad activity, if they ever existed, are yet to be found.

What, then, can we say tonight of Thomas Garrett? This is not the place to offer a eulogy such as that which was preached on the hundredth anniversary of his birth by William P. Tilden, pastor of the first Unitarian Church. We can, however, review briefly the story

of his life, for those to whom the details are not entirely familiar.   In
the telling we may add a little that is new.

Thomas Garrett was born of Quaker parents on a farm in Upper
Darby, Pennsylvania, in 1789.   In 1822 he moved to Wilmington and
went into the iron business.   As a merchant he was generally successful, although financial reverses and a heavy fine resulting from a
prosecution under the Fugitive Slave Law in 1848, practically bank-
rupted him.   He was able, however, to re-establish himself, even at
sixty years of age, and was comfortably well-to-do when he died in
1871.   In death he was honored by his fellow citizens, white and black
alike.   They filled the old meetinghouse on West Street to overflowing
at the funeral, joining in tribute to a man whom all respected and whom
many, particularly the Negroes, devotedly loved.[4]

The successful career of Thomas Garrett as a merchant brought
him respect, but it was his avocation of assisting fugitive slaves which
inspired devotion.   Garrett's Quaker heritage included a strong an-
tipathy to slavery, for the years of his youth coincided with the time
when the Society of Friends finally awakened to the irreconcilability
of slaveholding and Quakerism.   When Thomas Garrett was a boy,
Friends were occupied in attacking slavery in the state legislatures,
agitating for the prohibition of the African slave trade, and assisting
free Negroes who were unlawfully deprived of their liberty. Tradition
has it that a Negro woman in the employ of Thomas Garrett's father
was kidnapped by slave traders.   Thomas, then a man in his middle
twenties, traced the kidnappers from Darby to the Navy Yard and
thence to Kensington.   The story doesn't tell definitely whether or
not he was able to rescue the poor Negress.   He experienced, however,
a kind of road-to-Damascus vision of the sinfulness of slavery, and
received what he afterwards felt to be a call to devote his life to assisting its blameless victims.

Subsequent residence in Wilmington, in a slave State, gave him
ample opportunity to obey his call.   He became generally known as a
friend of fugitives, and his house as a place where fleeing Negroes might
find comfort and aid on their journey.   They came individually and in
families, most of them from Maryland and lower Delaware.   Their
number increased with the years.[5]

It should be remarked that Thomas Garrett, like most Quaker
operators on the Railroad, did not entice slaves to leave their masters.

The practice of enticement or abduction of Southern slaves was not rare among free Negroes, and a few white people engaged in it. Harriet Tubman, an escaped slave herself, became known as the Moses of her people by reason of her skillful excursions into the land of bondage. Her nineteen trips are said to have resulted in the emancipation of some three hundred slaves. Calvin Fairbanks, a white man similarly engaged in the enticement of Southern Negroes, was less successful than Harriet Tubman in evading detection. He was arrested several times and spent some seventeen years of his life in prison. He claimed after his release that he received thirty-five thousand stripes while serving a fifteen-year sentence in the Kentucky penitentiary. Fairbanks' case was unusual, however. The majority of the Underground Railroad operators limited their activity to obeying the Scriptural injunction to feed the hungry and clothe the naked. If they needed any excuse for their deeds, they believed they had ample religious sanction in the Golden Rule and political justification in the Declaration of Independence.

Naturally, however, there were many people in the slave State of Delaware who disagreed with Thomas Garrett and his fellow railroaders. Custom and the Constitution sanctioned slavery. Federal and local law made it a crime to assist a runaway slave. Many Wilmingtonians censured Thomas Garrett's activity as dangerous to the community and destructive of the Union. Others supported him tacitly, but few joined him in the work.* Ordinary men were unwilling to assume the serious risks involved.

Thomas Garrett was no ordinary man. He was courageous, capable, and shrewd, and above all he was convinced of the righteousness of his cause. It was no subtle religious philosophy which moved him, for he was not a subtle theologian. When once asked by an anxious religionist if he really believed "something," he replied, "Oh, yes, I do believe something. I believe in doing my duty. A man's duty is shown to him, and I believe in doing it, the first duty first and so on right along every time."[6] This simple formula provides the key to Thomas Garrett's character and activity. He believed that slavery was an evil. He had no alternative but to do his duty, which was to destroy it. The most convenient and congenial way he could find to accomplish this was to assist runaway slaves, regardless of the consequences. He never suffered personal injury in the work, although he

*It is notable that Siebert discovered only eight Underground Railway operators in Delaware besides Thomas Garrett: Isaac S. Flint, William Hardcastle, Ezekiel Hunn, John Hunn, Joseph G. Walker, and Benjamin, Thomas, and William Webb.—Siebert, *Underground Railroad*, p. 117, and Appendix E, p. 403.

was often threatened by slaveholders and their sympathizers. In January, 1860, in the ominous lull that preceded the storm of civil war, a resolution was introduced in the Maryland legislature, proposing a reward for his arrest on the general charge of slave stealing.[7] But Thomas Garrett's outspoken statement of his convictions seems to have over-awed his foes, for he braved this threat without difficulty, just as he had more than once exposed himself to the slaveholders' vengeance by journeys in the enemy country of southern Delaware and even South Carolina. He fairly stormed the citadel by announcing himself and his convictions in a firm if not a provocative manner. The disarming candor of his personality seems to have won the respect if not the agreement of his opponents.[8] His calm in the face of the Maryland resolution of 1860 is evident from a letter written to some Quaker friends in Pennsylvania:

"I write to say I note [that I have] not yet been kid-napped, by the Marylanders and I hope by this time my friends may breathe freer. I have had sundry letters from friends, some advising me to leave home for a few weeks, and one to go to England for a year or two, and take my wife along. I presume you have not been so much alarmed about me, it is true the papers have made free with my name, but I have given myself no trouble about what has been said until yesterday. I wrote a Statement of my position respect-ing aiding Slaves and sent it to the Peninsular News for in-sertion. . . Much love to you. [Signed] T. and R. Garrett."[9]

On one occasion, however, Thomas Garrett's shrewdly calculated good luck failed him. In 1848 two Marylanders, whose slaves he had sent to freedom on the Underground, pierced the armor of legality in which he usually cloaked his illegal operations. Their victory cost him dear. The true facts of the case have been somewhat obscured by conflicting evidence, but the essentials are these: A Negro couple and their six children appeared early one morning in late November, 1845, at the farm of John Hunn, the agent near Middletown, and asked for shelter after an all-night ride in a snow storm. During the course of the day a group of local men, with an eye to the captor's reward, asked to see the Negroes and insisted that they were runaways. In spite of the vigorous protests of the father, one Samuel Hawkins, that only two of the party were slaves, all were taken to the New Castle jail. At this point in the affair Thomas Garrett was notified of the trouble and went to New Castle to investigate. He was convinced of the truth of Hawkins' story, and, discovering that the commitments were defectively drawn up, determined to free the family if he could. With the assistance of his lawyer, John Wales, of Wilmington, he took them before Chief Justice Booth, and secured their release on a writ of habeas corpus. Thereupon, acting in humanity if not in wisdom, he secured a carriage and conveyed the eight grateful Negroes to his store in Wilmington. From there he sent them to Philadelphia, where another Quaker placed them in a safe and comfortable situation, out of reach of their former masters.

The two owners brought suit for damages against both John Hunn and Thomas Garrett. One, Charles W. Glanding, sought reimbursement for the loss of the two oldest Hawkins boys, whom the father had admitted were slaves. The other, widow Elizabeth N. Turner, claimed the mother and the four younger children, a claim which Hawkins had vehemently denied. The trial occurred in May, 1848, in the United States Circuit Court at New Castle, before Justice Hall and Chief Justice Roger B. Taney, later of Dred Scott fame. The court was obviously pro-slavery; local rumor had it that the jurors were equally so, and blamed the federal marshal for packing the jury. But Hunn and Garrett were probably guilty under the law. Lawyer James A. Bayard of Wilmington pleaded the case successfully against James Wales, Garrett's lawyer. Hunn was assessed damages of $2500., and Garrett $5400. Garrett's personal property was sold by the sheriff to recover for the plaintiffs. He lost practically everything he had. Undaunted, he continued his Underground Railroad activity, and was able, with the assistance of friends, both colored and white, to set himself up again in business.*

The significance of this trial was not lost upon the Delaware public. Years of abolitionist agitation in the Northern press and anti-slavery petitions in Congress had made the slavery issue a live one, and the Mexican War and the Wilmot Proviso had revived the bitter controversy over slavery in the Territories. The local *Delaware Gazette*, a Democratic paper with Southern leanings, ignored the Garrett-Hunn case until the damages were assessed, and then publicized it under the title "HARBORING SLAVES—HEAVY PENALTIES." The editors, one of whom, curiously enough, was named

---

*Varying accounts of the trial are given in Siebert, Still, and private manuscript sources. See also the records of the United States Circuit Court of Equity and Law for the May term, 1848, in the Clerk's office in Wilmington. Reports and comments on the trial appeared in Wilmington newspapers of the day, particularly in the *Blue Hen's Chicken*, a "Democratic-Whig" paper of abolitionist leanings, June 2, 1848, and continued.

William Penn Chandler, expressed themselves curtly but feelingly, "We hope that this severe punishment would remove the rails from the 'underground railway'."[10] In contrast to this, the *Blue Hen's Chicken*, a Whig paper supporting Clay's perennial hopes for the presidency, gave a great deal of space to the trial, opening its columns to Garrett and Hunn for long expositions of their defense. The editors of the "Chicken," as the paper was commonly called, upheld the motives and the actions of the defendants, saying:

> "If slavery is permitted to ruin and oppress our best citizens it is time something was done to remedy the evil. . . . We are no abolitionists, in the offensive sense of the word— that is we do not uphold or advocate any interference with slavery in the states where it is tolerated, but we are American citizens—we are republicans—democrats, if you please— whigs if you choose, or even democratic whigs; and we are opposed to slavery extension as we suppose every true hearted enlightened man is. And we abhor laws which will punish good men for humanity's sake; and we believe nine tenths of the good people of Delaware, whether slave-holders or not, deprecate the abominations of slavery. The slave catchers and slave-dealers are despicable characters; but he who has slaves of necessity, by decent or honest purchase, in slave states, and who treats them well is not to be condemned or abused, but are to be pitied for their misfortune and not to be condemned for their humanity, in making their condition as comfortable as possible. We go for abolition in Delaware upon fair and honorable terms—for the benefit of masters, and the state at large, even more than the slave; they should have freedom to be sure, which is sweet to every one bearing the image of man, but they would not be any better fed and clothed probably. Their children, however, might become more intelligent and thrifty. Free Delaware would become the garden spot of states, as she now is the pet among her sisters."[11]

Thomas Garrett's letter to the paper, embodying a speech he had made to the courtroom at the conclusion of his trial, indicated that to him the whole proceedings simply demonstrated the evil of slavery and the necessity of eliminating it. After proving his innocence, as he saw it, he alluded proudly to his twenty-five years as an abolitionist, and pledged himself to increased effort in the future, never to cease "while blessed with health and a slave remains to tread the soil of the State of my adoption—Delaware." He felt, however, that the value of the verdict for the anti-slavery cause would far outweigh the immediate advantages to slaveholders and the slave system, for reports would be published far and wide in the North, arousing a people already stirring with resentment against the "Slave Power." He believed that a final reckoning was not far distant, and that slavery would have to go or the Union would be dissolved. "The cause of freedom is progressing with rail road speed," he asserted. "I have not correctly read the signs of the times—if the days of slavery are not numbered in this country, the south will have to yield to the growing anti-slavery feeling of the north and west; or before ten years from this date there will be a dissolution of this Union—there is a point of forbearance beyond which the north and rapidly growing west will not submit."[12] In this prediction of the downfall of the slave system Thomas Garrett voiced the hope of many abolitionists. Little did he dream, we may hazard, that his prophecy of the break-up of the Union erred by only two brief years.

Thomas Garrett redoubled his work in the Underground Railroad, in spite of the inclusion of a more stringent Fugitive Slave Law in the Compromise of 1850. Traffic on the road increased generally, for the new law created greater anti-slavery sentiment in the North, and increased the determination of the Underground people to continue their effective boring from within. In the previous twenty-five years of his work on the Railroad, Thomas Garrett's passenger list had reached 1800. In the remaining twelve years before the government "went into the business wholesale," as he described the civil-war emancipation, he shipped over 900 more fugitives to places of safety in the free States or in Canada. Selections from his correspondence during the 'fifties, as published by William Still, show him sending to the Philadelphia anti-slavery office a single group of twenty-one men and women in 1855. Again, in 1856, he sought winter employment for four South Carolina Negro artisans who had fled to Wilmington by boat. The following year he wrote Still that he was sending "four of God's poor" to Philadelphia, and inquired as to the safe arrival of seven whom he had just sent ten days before.[13]

In spite of this intense preoccupation with assisting slaves to escape their bondage, Thomas Garrett's humanitarian feelings extended to white men who unwisely got into trouble in connection with a practice that was essentially the reverse of the Underground Railroad, namely, the organized kidnapping of free Negroes for sale in the Southern market. One Isaac Updike was convicted of kidnapping in 1846-47 in Wilmington, Thomas Garrett having spent a considerable amount of time and money in securing the conviction. In August, 1847, however, Garrett was moved by pity of Updike's condition and that of his needy family to seek a governor's pardon from the remainder of the sentence of lashes, fine, and two years in jail. Pleading that Updike had been shown to be a dupe of a gang of kidnappers, and that he had now received sufficient punishment for his ignorance and folly, Thomas Garrett secured thirty-eight signatures to a petition for a pardon. Updike was surprised and gratified at this friendly act of a former enemy, as appears in the appreciative if illiterate letter which he wrote to Garrett when informed of the prospective move to obtain a pardon.* The governor was not persuaded to grant the petition, unhappily for poor Updike, but the incident shows the breadth of Thomas Garrett's sympathy for unfortunate human beings, no matter what their color.

This excursion into aid for a repentant kidnapper was but a minor incident in Thomas Garrett's busy life. His real career was in helping slaves. For this he was honored by everyone when the Civil War united the cause of the Union with that of the abolitionists. In his own words he became "respectable," somewhat to his own amusement and even regret, regret that the exciting Railroad days were over. He was venerated by all in his declining years. The Wilmington *Daily Commercial* asserted at his death in 1871 that Thomas Garrett was more widely known, outside the city, than any other Wilmington man.[14] He had lived vigorously and he died peacefully in the consolation of a great work brought to a successful conclusion.

We may well admire the character and courage of Thomas Garrett in his determined struggle to right what is now universally regarded

---

*Garrett's correspondence with Updike and the governor are in the Delaware State Archives. The extract below is from a copy in private possession:

August 7th, 1847.

Mr. Garrett

  Sir I received your letter a few days ago an was not a little surprized to receive a letter from you. you talk as if you could get me out which if you can do I will be very much oblige to you for winter is a coming on and I would like to make some money before it sits in. it makes me feel grateful to think that I have one friend and one which I took to be my enemy. and if you succeed in getting me out of jaol I will be truly greateful for my wife and children have no other means of support than through my hard labour and if I am kept hear I am afraid the will suffer very much.

Yours Truly
Isaac Updike

as a wrong. The slavery question was not as simple in his generation, however, as it now seems to us. Underground Railroad activity was contrary to the federal constitution, to federal and state law, and to the property rights and the firm convictions of many good Americans. Thomas Garrett, in facing the dilemma of moral right versus legal right, denounced the law and circumvented it by every peaceful means in his power.

In attacking slavery by means of the Underground Railroad, Thomas Garrett raised another dilemma, particularly for a Quaker professing non-violence. For the Railroad carried the country toward sectional strife almost as directly as it carried slaves to Canada. Professor Siebert concluded his study of the Railroad with the assertion that it "was one of the greatest forces which brought on the Civil War, and thus destroyed slavery." Destroyed slavery? Yes. But at the cost of four years of war! The Underground was not alone responsible for the war, of course. But to the extent that it was responsible, the price of emancipation in blood and treasure was a heavy price to pay.

The degree to which Thomas Garrett understood the possible ramifications of his anti slavery enterprise is difficult to determine. His 1848 prediction of an eventual separation of the sections foresaw a peaceful secession of North and West. When secession came, it was the South that left the Union and was recalled by force of arms. Thomas Garrett and his fellow Quakers took no active part in the war. But as it became evident that Negro emancipation would result from Northern victory, Garrett's sympathy with Northern war aims was little disguised. On January 23, 1864, he sent a colored recruit to William Still, writing as follows:[16]

> "Respected Friend, William Still:—The bearer of this, Winlock Clark, has lately been most unrighteously sold for seven years, and is desirous of enlisting, and becoming one of Uncle Sam's boys; I have advised him to call on thee so that no land sharks shall get any bounty for enlisting him; he has a wife and several children, and whatever bounty the government or the State allows him, will be of use to his family. Please write me when he is snugly fixed in his regimentals, so that I may send word to his wife. By so doing, thee will much oblige thy friend, and the friend of humanity,
>
> THOMAS GARRETT."

As a postscript he added:

"N. B.   Am I naughty, being a professed non-resistant, to advise this poor fellow to serve Father Abraham?   T. G."

The problem of this "friend of humanity" as he called himself, in reconciling humanity's battles with the Quaker principle of peace is in this postscript.   We sympathize with Thomas Garrett as he wrestled with the problem.   We join him in regretting that a civil war should have been the terrible dénouement of his humanitarian crusade.   We rejoice with him in the freeing of the slaves.

REFERENCES

[1] Wilbur H. Siebert, *The Underground Railroad from Slavery to Fredom* (New York, The Macmillan Company, 1898), pp. 110-111 *et passim.*

[2] William Still, *Underground Railroad Records* (First edition, 1872; revised edition, Philadelphia, published by the author, 1883), pp. 623-641 *et passim.* References in this paper are to the 1886 reprint of the 1883 revision.

[3] Information supplied by inquiry of Mr. John M. Mendinhall, Wilmington, March 18, 1938.

[4] Newspaper reports of the funeral, reprinted in William Still, *Underground Railroad Records* (Revised edition, 1886), pp. 627-630.

[5] William P. Tilden, *Thomas Garrett, a Memorial Address, 1889* (Privately printed, 1935), p. 7.

[6] Tilden, *Thomas Garrett,* p. 11.

[7] Siebert, *Underground Railroad,* p. 53.

[8] Manuscript in private possession.

[9] Letter to Isaac and Dinah Mendenhall and Joseph and Ruth Dugdale, dated Wilmington, Second month 7, 1860, preserved in the Delaware State Archives. This extract is from a copy in private possession.

[10] *Delaware Gazette* (Wilmington), June 30, 1848.

[11] *Blue Hen's Chicken* (Wilmington), June 2 and 9, 1848. The grammar and spelling are the *Chicken's* own.

[12] *Ibid.,* June 9, 1848.

[13] Still, *Underground Railroad Records* (1886), pp. 637-640.

[14] *Wilmington Daily Commercial,* January 25, 1871.

[15] Still, *Underground Railroad Records* (1886), p. 641.

JOHN DICKINSON:
Character of a Revolutionist*

John H. Powell

JOHN DICKINSON, 1732-1808

IT IS the biographer's fate to concern himself with the trivial, to deal in the minutiae of personality which can rarely be attractive to those who study results rather than struggles. And so, while this Society devotes a portion of its anniversary program to a consideration of the career of John Dickinson, I am forced in a somewhat trivial manner to pause over the question, was Dickinson a Friend? This matter has been much discussed, but I have found no reason to differ from the conclusion of President Sharpless, namely, that if he was not actually a member of the Meeting, he did nevertheless hold many opinions which were agreeable to Quaker philosophy.

More specifically the following facts may be noted: Dickinson's paternal grandfather (who may have been an Anglican) married into a family which was the very nucleus of early Quakerism on the Eastern Shore of Maryland. His father, Samuel Dickinson, was reared in the Meeting, but he was disciplined (though not disowned) by the Quarterly Meeting for consenting to his daughter's marriage outside the Society, and some cloud appears to have hung over him after this affair, for when he moved from Maryland to Delaware the Third Haven Friends wrote letters commending his wife, but avoided all mention of him. Dickinson's birthright through his father is thus not entirely clear, but his mother, Mary Cadwalader, was a vigorous and devout participant in the Philadelphia

(87)

* Address presented at the Bicentennial Celebration of the Wilmington Monthly Meetings of Friends.

Meeting, and as long as he remained under his mother's influence Dickinson was almost certainly schooled in Quakerism.

But as soon as they left their father's Delaware plantation both he and his brother Philemon (later a military leader) seem to have become indifferent to the Meeting. Between the years 1757 and 1776 Dickinson had no religious connection with the Quakers and strongly opposed them politically. He did not in this period use the intimate form of address in his letters. In 1770, however, he married Mary Norris, whose membership may have turned him back somewhat, and in 1785, when he retired to this city, he began a study of theological principles which was to occupy him for the remaining twenty years of his life. He then took part in the Wilmington Meeting, instructed his daughters in Quaker tenets, and expressed his desire to be buried in the Meetinghouse yard.

So in different degrees and at different times, the Society of Friends had its influence upon Dickinson's thought. It was one sort of experience which contributed to the formation of his character. I wish to take this occasion to speak of a few other personal aspects of his career, in the hope that I may suggest some explanations of the manner in which he met the critical issues of his day.

II

In considering the personality of John Dickinson due weight must be given to that habit of thought, universal in the eighteenth century, of moralizing upon the literature of the past. It is especially important in the case of a writer who leaned so heavily upon his learning as Dickinson did. Like his contemporaries, he sought in his reading rules of conduct, standards of judgment, that in the absence of formal educational institutions could be derived nowhere else. He studied history for the lessons it had to give him, conceived parallel situations, sought to profit by previous examples. He discovered in his "many weighty authors" ideas which buttressed his arguments and quickened his beliefs. For him a knowledge of the classics—the most acceptable referent of his century—was valued not because it was an elegant achievement of a gentleman, but because it enabled him to add to his own contentions the prestige of ancient authority. He read with a purpose: this he had been taught to do in the best tradition of the century. It was a habit he had developed early in life. A common-

place book kept during his boyhood has come down to us, in which the
desire to gather up and catalogue principles of good behaviour, rules
for achieving virtue, moral lessons of all kinds is expressed. He
excised passages from his voracious reading and grouped them under
such headings as Conscience, Criticism, Fame, Love, Liberty, Government, Justice, Virtue and Vice. Constantly in his mature pamphleteer-
ing, also, he adduced laws from history by which to test present issues,
or construed the problem of the day as a modern instance of something
which had occurred before. His interest in the struggles of his own
time governed his selections of lessons from history, and his moral sense
assured their survival in his thought.

III

But while vicariously seeking the experience of others through
his books, Dickinson was having experiences of his own which were
important in shaping his political instincts. It is not without significance, for example, that as the proprietor of a huge estate he was
continually dealing with a large group of tenants. Much of his time and
energy was spent in writing leases and renewals of leases, in authorizing
the building of fences, the draining of swamps, the erection of barns,
and those thousand and one details that the owner of land must look
to. Documents concerning such matters represent by far the largest
number of manuscripts which survive from his pen. In the midst of
a critical election he must turn his attention to listing the cows, horses,
mules, sheep and hogs on a remote Maryland plantation. From ad-
dressing the Supreme Executive Council of Pennsylvania he must
retire to his study to send a soothing letter to his litigious Delaware
neighbor, Thomas Rodney. Before attending the Federal Convention
on a hot July morning he must dispatch instructions to his Kent County
agents by the impatient courier. From his retirement in Wilmington
he must journey to Philadelphia to dicker with the insurance company
over a house which has burnt. He must deal with hundreds of incidents, vignettes of human experience, which contain both tragedy and
comedy in the brief glimpses they give us into his affairs. Mary Hays
widow, has been put off the land she had supposed Dickinson's two
weeks after her husband's death by a man claiming to be the new
owner; she writes for advice and help: ". . . now I have neither
house nor home to put my head in now I have nothing to trust to but
the Almighty God and your honour . . ." Deborah White, also

Upper by Ellwood Garrett

JOHN DICKINSON'S HOUSE 1860

WILLIAM SHIPLEY HOUSE

a widow, petitions during a crucial, much publicized slavery controversy at a time when attention is focussed on Dickinson's attitude: she wishes to clear land for a turnip-field, but the negroes will not obey her; the peach orchard is a den of thieves, her slaves insubordinate: "If the old Blacks say that I Picked the Woll I offered them it is notorious false for I weighed all the woll that Come off the Sheep Except three fleecis to make their Compliment which I never opened to See Whether it was good or bad . . ."

Here Dickinson was meeting with many types of people, learning the vernacular in thought and expression of widely separated communities, equipping himself for the task of popular writing. He never got far away from the agricultural life, nor did he ever lose his conviction that a rural population was the finest foundation that could be laid "for the secure establishment of civil liberty and national independence." It was not unfitting that his greatest work should open with the words, "I am a Farmer . . ."

IV

A third aspect deserves comment: that is, his interest as a lawyer. Dickinson began his legal career at a propitious moment, for the Philadelphia bar was just at that time beginning to grow. Between 1741 and the year of independence one hundred thirty-two lawyers are known to have been admitted to practice before the various courts of the province. This new generation to which Dickinson belonged was remarkable in several respects. Its size testified to the demand in Pennsylvania for a system of law which would meet changing conditions of a developing society. The presence of men from other provinces indicated the increasing complexity of intercolonial relationships, and the number from towns other than Philadelphia portrayed the growth of western communities.

Thus Dickinson entered the law at a time when a lively legal profession responsible only to itself was arising, when a strong and independent bench of judges appointed from that profession was appearing, and when a close partnership between the lawyers and the legislative bodies was beginning to be accepted. A legal profession was a relatively new phenomenon in American life; it was to play a major role in the next half-century.

The legal aspects of Dickinson's thought are clearly apparent in his constant plea for a liberty guaranteed by a known and certain law; they are also revealed by his repeated attention to constitutional arguments, by his desire to define and preserve the institutions which had evolved from two centuries of imperial practice, by his study of common law writers. To these he added a period of English study which instructed him in the Whig theories of the British government.

But the law gave him another sort of experience which is more important for our purposes. His continuance dockets and account books list some of the thousands of cases with which he dealt; they picture the endless stream of people of all sorts and classes which flowed through his office—people from whom Dickinson learned much concerning the political and social problems with which he was to deal. His knowledge gained from these contacts broadened his frame of reference, and when, in 1765, he discussed the plight of the "lower ranks of the people" he was speaking from personal observation.

V

Dickinson's three years in London had increased his skill in the law; they had also brought him into close touch with his English business agents, the Quaker firm Osgood Hanbury & Co. In the formation of his ideas concerning the Empire this relationship played an interesting part.

It influenced his life in two ways. First, he was obligated to his factors for many of those commodities which made his elegant standard of living famous in Philadelphia. At his request Hanbury would go round among the shops purchasing such goods as carpeting, glassware, china, silk hose, shoe knots, fur muffs and tippets, herring bone for servants' clothing, papier maché bottle stands, blankets and furniture. On one occasion he ordered one silver chafing dish, one "very best Gold Horizontal Watch cap'd Jewel'd & chand £32-10," with a "Gold chain for same," one bronze bust of Chatham and a pair of mahogany andirons. Through Hanbury he also filled up his wine cellar, purchasing usually twelve dozen bottles at a time.

Dependent upon the English merchant for those goods which were not to be had in America, and relying upon him for the sale of his plantations' produce, Dickinson also conducted his financial operations through the Hanburys. These operations were not particularly large, but by the incidents of commerce they extended Dickinson's correspondence widely throughout the Empire. His wealth in terms of lands and credits was considerable, but it was not always mobile. There were times when he, as even the richest men in the colonies, was embarrassed by the movements of exchange and the necessary delays in communicating with his London factors. Demands for "the earliest Intelligence" were frequent. A good example of what might occur is the following story. Cadwalader Morris, a cousin of John Dickinson, planned a trip as super-cargo to the West Indies. He made a business arrangement with Dickinson before he set out, and Dickinson, advising Hanbury that Morris might command him to the extent of five hundred pounds, asked that his bills be paid. When Morris reached the Islands he drew upon his credit with Hanbury, but before he left he had enough cash to pay the debt at once. He announced his intention of doing so in a letter to Dickinson. When this letter reached him Dickinson was in need of cash. He therefore seized the opportunity to borrow 400 odd pounds from a local merchant, one John Gibson, giving him an order on Hanbury for the amount. He wrote to London: "If, by any Accident, Mr. Morris shall not replace the Money when Mr. Gibson's Bills become payable, I beg the Favor of You to honor them, being assur'd that You will receive the Money in a few Days ..." Several months passed, and Gibson's demands turned up in Hanbury's office. For one reason or another Morris had failed to make good his promise, and Dickinson stood in his agent's debt to the extent of nearly a thousand pounds on this one casual transaction. Hanbury wrote Dickinson to inform him of the default, but his letter crossed with one of Dickinson, who had been surprised to receive not a canceled bill but a further demand from the sanguine Morris. This liberty caught him after a successful crop had been sold, and he was in funds. He dispatched to London a bill in favor of Morris drawn on James Burnett at Jamaica, wrote to Morris to secure endorsements of his notes, and applied to his brother in Philadelphia, S. L. Morris, for a guaranty that the five hundred pounds should be paid.

This was a routine transaction of the sort in which Dickinson's funds were constantly tied up. It would be tedious to recount any more such; the point has been sufficiently illustrated that through his business operations Dickinson's interests were disseminated through many of the British occidental colonies. He had a stake in the commercial success of enterprises in Jamaica, Barbados, Nova Scotia, and England herself, as well as in Pennsylvania. It cannot be doubted that his imagination, wandering after his pocket-book, gave him a feeling of the inter-relations among the provinces; it may have been this as much as anything which enabled him in the 60's and 70's to look beyond the immediate local problems to the advantages derived from the protected trade of the colonial system. It would have been strange had he not sought to preserve the Empire, for the Empire was contained in his ledgers and daybooks.

VI

These aspects of his personal life, therefore, had a certain effect upon Dickinson's political and social thought, and they must be taken into account in treating of his part in the American Revolution. Confronted by that great period, the writer who concerns himself with the education and reading, the agricultural and legal preoccupations, the English correspondence and business engagements of one man may seem to deal in matters of such special interest that they have no other meaning than that of antiquarian lore of a research worker. He does, however, have his reward, for he is seeking to understand through the help of one not unimportant character a movement which was after all an important personal experience to those who took part in it. Our knowledge will be increased if we can come to appreciate the forces which moved the men of the Revolutionary generation to do what they did.

It may be added, that those classical concepts of civic virtue which dominated the eighteenth century have a lesson for us. Dickinson was propelled by every phase of his training and his career to fight against innovation whether it came from Pennsylvania leaders or from the English parliament. His opinions were conservative, and in their conservatism represented the interests of his busy life. One of these interests was expressed by his continual reiteration of the need for integrity and calm judgment in public administration.

When first elected to the Pennsylvania Assembly (in his thirtieth year) he wrote to a friend: "I flatter myself that I come in with the approval of all good men. I confess, that I should like to make an immense bustle in the world, if it could be done by virtuous actions; but, as there is no probability in that, I am content if I can live innocent and beloved by those I love." And on the title page of his first published tract he inserted a quotation from Sallust: "As for me, I will assuredly contend for that glorious plan of Liberty handed down to us from our ancestors . . ." In the same vein, and reminiscent of his Roman studies, was his judgment concerning the peace of 1763: "No Doubt We shall make an immensely advantageous or rather gainful Peace—Our Commerce will be incredible—Our Riches exorbitant—Our Luxury embroidered—Our Corruption in Time universal—& our Ruin,—certain. Such seems the inevitable Fate of Empires—the Consequences of Success—the Fruits of Glory—But unborn Events of such distant Ages—appear not related to Us—Tho they ought to teach Us Virtue, Humility & Humanity."

From a person who thought in such terms as these it is worth noting for our present edification a remark evoked by the view of European politics in 1800. Considering the tyranny of the absolute rulers of that day, the challenge they presented to the new American ideal of republicanism, Dickinson exclaimed: "Noble princes! Friends of Mankind! In their lives may there be peace, and in their Deaths—HOPE!" There springs to mind the grateful thanks of the seventeenth century cleric, freed from the disabilities of Stuart tyranny: "We ought to be glad, when those that are fit for government, are called to it, are willing to take the burden of it upon them . . ."

"A good man," Dickinson once asserted, "ought to serve his country, even though she resents his services."

THE FRIENDS MEETING HOUSE, FOURTH AND WEST STREETS - 6TH MO. 5TH, 1938   *Brooks Studio*

OUR LINK IN THE QUAKER CHAIN*

William W. Comfort

IT HAS been suggested by the committee in charge of this anniversary celebration that the President of Friends Historical Association should indulge in a glance forward into the future of the Society of Friends. This proposal affords an unusual opportunity for anyone whose function it is to deal largely with the Past. Being neither a prophet myself nor possessing any prophetic ancestors, I shall not pretend to look through any private keyhole into the future, but shall only comment briefly upon one detail of the prospect before us as anyone may see it. Even that much of a preview of the future may afford us something sufficiently interesting and important to warrant our attention upon such an occasion.

In general, it is true that the future will be what our descendants make it. But those of us who are concerned for Quakerism know that what our children will think of it depends upon what we make of it now. So without prophesying what it will be, we may indicate what we ought to be doing now in order to discharge our responsibility for the future. We must play our part now. " 'I think every man would like to come of an ancient and honorable race,' said Colonel Newcombe to Clive in his honest way. 'As you like your father to be an honorable man, why not your grandfather, and his ancestors before him? But if we can't inherit a good name, at least we can do our best to leave one, my boy; and that is an ambition which, please God, you and I will both hold by'."

As Friends, we have inherited a good name, but we also have to leave one. There is still plenty to do. The hopes of the fathers have not all been fulfilled. We cannot close the account book of either past revelation or of our present duty. One is wrapped up in the other. We cannot conjugate the verb of the Society's existence only in the past tenses: there are also present and future tenses to be learned. This is what the author of the Epistle to the Hebrews had to say to his Jewish contemporaries, expressed in words pregnant with meaning for us today. After reviewing the heroes of Israel, their sufferings and death for their religion, he continues: "These all, having obtained a

(97)

_____

*Address presented at the Bicentennial Celebration of the Wilmington Monthly Meeting of Friends.

good report through faith, received not the promise, God having provided some better thing for us, that they without us should not be made perfect. Wherefore, seeing we also are compassed about with so great a cloud of witnesses, let us lay aside every weight and the sin which doth so easily beset us, and let us run with patience the race that is set before us." You know the rest of the passage and you see what large applications of this appeal could be made here today, if this were the time and place for a prophetic and evangelical message.

But the fact is that Eastern Quakerism has today quite renounced a prophetic or evangelical ministry in favor of a social gospel. It is the moral and social implications of Quakerism which have captivated us and directed our activity in the neighboring Yearly Meetings. With the years, and increasingly so of late, our Quaker interpretation of duty has passed into philanthropic lines, into effective committees and organizations formed to deal with the social and economic woes of a stricken world. If, to make clear what we mean, we use the words now current, we must admit that the practical side of Quakerism is far better staffed and interpreted than the mystical side.

Among our purely secular characteristics, the most striking are our social solidarity and our experience as philanthropists. Except in my capacity as an official in an historical society, I do not regret the passing of the picturesque badges which formerly set us apart in the street. But the social solidarity and the experience in philanthropy are two precious assets. It may be doubted, however, if they can be preserved unless we put first the meeting for worship. That is the only place to put it. Every good and perfect gift which our Society possesses is predicated upon the meeting for worship and a live ministry in it. And our meetings for worship are no longer in first place. There are many Friends on the membership list who never go to meeting; there are too many others who go only when they have nothing else to do; and nine out of ten of those who do go have no intention of taking any responsibility for the spiritual life of the worshipping group: they go for sociability, from habit, from a sense of duty, or with a desire to be helped by the spiritual exercise of others; they contribute only vicariously by their presence, by their approval or their criticism of what others express.

Recent writers in our Society have plainly shown the way to revitalize our meetings for worship. It is not necessary to restate here their accurate specifications for spiritual worship in our Society. But there is time for comment upon what the trouble is. Perhaps it will do us good to recognize ourselves in what follows.

In a religious Society as small as ours there is only a limited amount of man-power. This available man-power is put to a heavy strain to maintain and direct all the institutions and concerns for which Friends have made themselves responsible. Schools, colleges, libraries, banks, hospitals, asylums, prisons, community charities, philanthropies both national and international—all require financial support and active personnel. As the years go by, it becomes a serious question whether we have not taken on more than we can efficiently manage. Not a few of our ablest members spend their days going from one board or committee to another. They have only a limited amount of energy. It is plainly evident that many of our most gifted and, from every point of view, most valued members, have not the time and perhaps not the energy to make any preparations for our meetings for worship. This is a misfortune, if not for them, surely for the rest of us. For there can be no doubt that the brief and simple exercises of such persons whom we know to be immersed in the heavy tide of life are quite as helpful to others as the more frequent and facile communications of those who have withdrawn from business or who never had any experience in the world of affairs. If many more of our 'lay' members, both men and women, from the middle benches felt their responsibility in the ministry, we should have enough and to spare for the opening of new and smaller meetings, without in the least depriving our larger meetings of the life to which they are entitled. Despite our profession of a free ministry, it may be doubted if in a given year five per cent of our membership appear in our meetings for worship either on their feet or on their knees. The unavowed tendency to set apart a small group of experienced persons and expect them to express the spiritual concern of the meeting tends to be fatal. It is the natural way, it is the easy way, but it is not the Quaker way and it has been shown over and over again to be the fatal way for Quakerism. It cuts the nerve of the only kind of apostolic succession in which we believe—the successive welling up in souls which are tendered afresh from time to time of those personal yearnings and disciplines which must be shared with others before they can be properly relieved and become effective.

The part of education in the encouragement of such a lay ministry is evident and has often been emphasized. Suffice it to say here that in a religious society where all are potential ministers, the average of intelligence must be higher than in a group where worship is somewhat vicariously exercised, and where a trained body of professionals minister to the spiritual needs of the group. Friends have a high reputation for their educational foundations. But they are by no means using to capacity the very institutions they have founded for their own youth. Too many Friends are sending their children either to public schools for financial reasons, or to non-Quaker colleges for social reasons. In such cases the children may receive an excellent intellectual education, but they are not exposed to any religious experience which can be mistaken for Quakerism. What the effect of this will be in the next generation we do not yet know, but it is well for Friends to be acquainted with this recent development in our midst. It may be feared that our youth is not so firmly rooted in the Quakerism of the home as to be able to withstand the effect of transplanting. Separation is only a step from alienation.

To return for a moment to our meetings for worship. Some of them are too small to develop any spontaneous vitality. Others are too large to permit the numerous attenders to feel personal responsibility. It would be ideal if there could be a division of our available membership on an approximately equal basis among the existent meetings in groups of twenty-five to fifty in any given assembly. Manifestly, any such solution is impossible. Here, however, is a practical suggestion: Meetings which are comparatively rich in numbers and spiritual power can extend their influence through regular and systematic visitation, concentrating their efforts upon one weak or closed meeting after another. This system has been successfully tried in more than one community. It can be tried elsewhere, where there is an unchurched group awaiting cultivation through a live ministry. Doubtless you have here within easy reach of Wilmington a number of meetings which have been laid down or which are moribund in rural surroundings. A group of young Friends would find it stimulating to hold meetings regularly in such places, to call on people in the countryside and invite their attendance by every legitimate appeal. If Quakerism has any genuine religion to offer, I believe that the response would be gratifying. Moreover, if our Society is to survive it must be recruited more effectualy than merely by our own birth rate. About forty-five persons were received last year in Arch Street

Yearly Meeting by convincement, approximately one per cent of the membership.

Much as our members can contribute through their leadership in local, national and international good works, they could contribute a still more unique service by maintaining spiritual power-houses where spirits may find peace, quiet and spiritual refreshment, where inspiration for these very forms of social relief may be gained, where in quiet and without the distraction of human contrivance, men may worship the great Spirit in spirit and in truth. It is to be feared that without constant repair to that source which alone can inspire and fructify our more secular activities, our Society may degenerate into a merely philanthropic and humanitarian association. Let us remember that we belong to the 'Religious Society of Friends.' When we are gathered as now in the impressive shadows of a long past, we may well take heed that we leave to our descendants of the next two centuries in these parts the living experience of a theory of worship which our ancestors knew and which underlies and undergirds all the other good works which may be built upon it. As Douglas V. Steere has recently reminded us, "This corporate ceremonial communion in any Christian group that is more than occasional in its character carries a sense of historical continuity with a great spiritual tradition. You do not begin this quest, nor will it end with you. It has been lived in the world of space and time by others who have gone before. . . . It is no mean asset to have and to be regularly reminded of what T. S. Eliot calls 'the backing of the dead.' " This it seems to me is the eternal message of the Past to the Future, this is the truth which warrants the existence of an historical society: the vital nerve which binds the Future with the Past.

Historians have so much of interest to tell us that they are apt to be gay and stirring in their recitals; prophets are often so depressed by the present world that they contemplate the future with dire forebodings. There is much in the past of Quakerism for which we may today give thanks, and those fundamental principles are as fresh and modern today as are those of any expression of religion in the world. There is nothing invalid or out of date about Quakerism. It is in tune with the most modern demands of religious psychology. That should be repeated again and again for the benefit of our youth. But the Society of Friends is not as potent as its doctrine is true.

And that is our fault. Some of the reasons for our spiritual impotence have been mentioned. The future will belong to our children, but the responsibility for what we leave them is ours.

A MEETING HOUSE MOUSE*

N THE old brick meeting house on the hill
Sat the silent worshippers—patient and still;
Men on this side, women on that,
In plaited bonnet and broad-brimmed hat.
Clad in garments of drab and gray,
All in the old-fashioned Quaker way;
Masculine figures sedate and demure,
Motherly presences mild and pure;
Shut off from the world with its shows and mocks,
As worthy disciples of good George Fox.

To those pious elders, thus hedged about
The silence with meaning was full, no doubt;
But to children, more active in body than brain,
With warm life bubbling in every vein,
Who rather than sit would run and climb,
Long and irksome was meeting time.

So thought two children, dear lovers of play,
In mid-week meeting sitting one day:—
Phoebe, fond of more fun and stir
Than girlish demureness could offer her;
Robby, not yet in his boyish pride
Disdaining to sit on the "Woman's-side."
Counting the laggard minutes crawl
As the shadows slid down the whitewashed wall.
Tracing the cracks in the oaken floor,
The nails that studded the heavy door;
Thinking, while hearing the breezes chime,
Of future frolics in chestnut times;
Or turning, these vagrant thoughts to stem,
To grandmother, sitting there facing them:—
Best of grandmothers! peacefully sitting
With hands at rest from her endles knitting
And dear calm face, where a still light shone
From a source to those restless ones unknown.

*A true episode.

But lo, in the corner behind the door
What little gray creature slides over the floor,
Can it be—yes, surely it is—a mouse
Astray from its kind, in the Meeting-house!
No, not one mouse only, either, but three;
One old and two little ones, plain to see;
The young ones cling close to the mother's sides
As this and that way she noiselessly glides,
Taking their dinner the self-same way
Young mammals have done since creation day.

Not dullness now, but a keen delight
Our urchins feel at so rare a sight.
Close presses a hand to each mouth and chin
To keep back the laughter bubbling within;
In gleeful attention two pairs of eyes
With eagerness widen to double size.
Watching the mouse-mother scan each spot,
Seeking a dinner where dinners are not.

But see; on the floor by grandmother's foot
What crumbs are scattered of cake or fruit?
From grandmother's pocket, no doubt, they fell;
That pocket so inexhaustible,
Where so many grandchildren, little and big,
Find cake or candy, almond or fig.

Mousey seeks not the source to guess
Of this manna spread in the wilderness.
She gathers the treat up every crumb,
Wishing only that more would come;
Then climbs to the top of grandmother's shoe,
Dragging the little ones with her, too.
And calmly, in sight of all in the place,
Trims her whiskers and washes her face.
'Tis plain she accounts these figures she sees
No more to be feared than a rind of cheese.

Not without warrant did mousey dare,
No harm for the harmless one was there.
None seemed to notice her, or at least,
None moved, none shrank from the little beast.

Only grandmother's mild eyes sweet
Dwelt on the little ones at her feet.
And the children fancied they saw a smile
Faintly dawn on her face the while.

The elders shood hands and the meeting was done;
The youngsters were free for their homeward run;
To rush, Robbie foremost, in haste to inquire
Of grandmother, snug by the sitting-room fire—
"Grandmother, how could thee sit so mute
When that funny old mouse ran over thy foot?
Why, the other day, how we heard thee squeal!
When one ran from under thy spinning wheel!
I guess thee thought that the elders would frown
To-day, so thee kept the squealing down.
But those two little mice were too cunning by half!
Grandmother, how could thee help but laugh?
One wee little smiling we saw begin
But thee pinched thy lips up and squeezed it in."

Grandmother smiled, without offense
At the heedless urchin's impertinence.
While with knitting needle from work removed
She pushed back the hair from the brow she loved.
" 'Tis silly," she said, "to be ever afraid
Of the innocent creatures that God has made;
But though I am silly thus sometimes, dear,
I felt no shrinking to-day nor fear;
And if I smiled! 'twas with deeper joy
Than thee thought, at the pretty sight, my boy.
I remembered the psalm where a promise is
Of a feast in the midst of our enemies,
And I saw how our Father's tender care
Is over his creatures everywhere;
How He without whom no sparrow can fall
Knows the food best fitted for one and all:—
For the soul which can worship and love and adore,
And the poor little mouse on the meeting-house floor."

Margaret C. Pyle

BICENTENNIAL CELEBRATION

Fifth Month, 14 and 15, 1938

Catharine Balderston Swift

THE Friends Historical Association of Philadelphia and the Friends' Meetings of Wilmington united in observing the two-hundredth anniversary of the founding of the Wilmington Friends Meeting. The committees were as follows:

GENERAL COMMITTEE OF WILMINGTON FRIENDS

John M. Mendinhall, *Chairman*, Wilmington, Delaware

A. Stanley Ayers	James R. Frorer	John Richardson, Jr.
Marjery Ayers	W. Ralph Gawthrop	Shermer H. Stradley
Isabel J. Booth	Enos J. Hollingsworth	Elizabeth R. Tatnall
Edward P. Bartlett	Alice Johnson	Horace J. Tatnall
Esther S. Chambers	Mary B. Passmore	Garrett Taylor
Walter A. Dew	William C. Philips	Anna M. Worth
	J. Edgar Rhoads	

FRIENDS HISTORICAL ASSOCIATION ENTERTAINMENT COMMITTEE

Lydia Glagg Gummere, *Chairman*, Haverford, Pennsylvania

Mary S. Allen	Anna B. Hewitt	George Vaux
Eliza R. Bishop	George N. Highley	Mary James Vaux
Linda W. Corson	Walter F. Price	Edward Woolman
Thomas E. Drake	Jane Moon Snipes	Lilian W. Woolman
Henry V. Gummere	Elizabeth T. Taylor	Lydia R. Woolman

The Seventh-day gathering was held at the new Friends School on Alapocas Drive. In spite of inclement weather, more than twelve hundred Friends and friends of Friends gathered to take part in the program of addresses and pageantry. The formal exercises, originally arranged for an outdoor stage, were transferred to the spacious school building where the large assembly was housed without confusion and without destroying the spirit of friendliness and joyousness which prevailed. A unique collection of old documents and articles of folk art of the early Quaker life and customs in Delaware was on display in cases in the halls and social room. The afternoon and evening sessions were in charge of acting chairman James R. Frorer.

PROGRAM OF EVENTS
2.45 P. M.

ADDRESS OF WELCOME

John M. Mendinhall, Chairman of the General Committee of Wilmington Friends.

HISTORICAL PAGEANT OF WILMINGTON FRIENDS MEETING

Members of the Meeting, First-day School, and Friends School

Episode I: Elizabeth Shipley's Dream and Her Visit to Wilmington, 1735.

Episode II: Scene from the First Friends School, 1748.

Episode III: First-day Meeting, Eighth Month, 1777.

Episode IV: The Female Benevolent Society, 1800.

Episode V: Thomas Garrett becomes an Abolitionist, about 1813.

Episode VI: The Social Lyceum, Second Month 3, 1873.

Episode VII: The Meeting and First-day School Carry On, 1868-1938.

Conclusion: Singing of "The Hymn of All Nations" by all present.

ADDRESS: OUR LINK IN THE QUAKER CHAIN

William W. Comfort, President of Friends Historical Association.

SUPPER

Those attending will provide their own box suppers; coffee and ice cream will be supplied by Wilmington Friends and the Friends Historical Association.

EVENING MEETING
7 P. M.

Chairman, William W. Comfort

RETROSPECT OF WILMINGTON FRIENDS

W. Ralph Gawthrop, *Wilmington, Delaware*

JOHN DICKINSON, 1732-1808, Quaker Signer of the Constitution

John H. Powell, *State University of Iowa*

THOMAS GARRETT, 1789-1871, Quaker Abolitionist

Thomas E. Drake, *Haverford College*

COMMEMORATIVE MEETING, Friends Meeting House, Fourth and West Streets, Wilmington.

FIRST-DAY MEETING
11 A. M.

COMMEMORATIVE MEETING, Friends Meeting House, Fourth and West Streets, Wilmington.

On First-day morning, the fifteenth, a commemorative meeting under the auspices of the two Monthly Meetings was held at the Fourth and West Streets Meeting House, with about three hundred twenty-five people in attendance. D. Elton Trueblood, of Stanford University, spoke at the opening of the meeting on the values of the past which should be guideposts for us in the present as well as for the future generations. Others who had vocal part in the meeting were Allen P. Clement, of Haddonfield, N. J., Walter W. Haviland, of Lansdowne, Pa., Francis R. Taylor, of Frankford, Pa., W. Ralph Gawthrop, of Wilmington, Del., Henry C. Ferris, of Germantown, Pa., William H. Richie, Jr., of Moorestown, N. J., and Esther Morton Smith, of Washington, D. C.

Many friends and former members met with us and the meeting was rich in real fellowship and spiritual communion. It was brought home to us that the lives of those gone before must be fulfilled in us who in turn must be the bridges between those lives and the generations to come.

ADDRESS OF WELCOME

John M. Mendinhall

It is a pleasant task given today to the Friends of Wilmington, in cooperation with the Friends' Historical Association, to welcome all visiting Friends and their friends to our gathering. It is not often that we can look backward two hundred years in connection with the institutions with which we are associated, and Wilmington Friends have felt this opportunity was so precious that we must take advantage of it to invite all of you to share it with us.

Those of you who are our neighbors from Wilmington, we are glad to welcome because our history and traditions have been so intertwined with yours that we cannot but feel that we are celebrating your history along with our own.

Those of you from out of the city, though still our neighbors over a wider circle, we are particularly glad to welcome not as strangers, but as Friends of the common ancestry in the Wider Fellowship of which we are all so proud. It is our hope that all our friends will feel free today not only to examine our new school on these grounds, but also to visit the Meeting Houses in the city which are open for your inspection.

It is only out of the past that building of the future can be accomplished. Accordingly, we feel it proper to remind everyone present that the celebration today was made possible only through the joint efforts of both Meetings in Wilmington. Both have shared jointly in all preparations.

While it is premature to quote the Minute adopted by the two Monthly Meetings, I cannot let this occasion slip by without letting you know that because of the very great benefit derived from the continual and ready cooperation between them, both our Meetings have committed themselves to the general policy of still closer communion in the future. We only hope that you are as thrilled by our being able to make this announcement as we are.

Just a word about the pageant that is to follow:

In the first place, both Meetings, the First-day School and Friends School all felt direct responsibility in its creation and presentation. Secondly, the episodes depicted are all events that grew out of the religious life of the Meeting. Thirdly, it is intersting to note how these important events of the Meetings always foreshadowed similar events in the life of the community, so that in many instances we are depicting today the development of our city and country.

The men and women Friends, as they take their places on the facing benches, will be in the costume of the day of the episode depicted.

I now take pleasure in presenting the Pageant of the Wilmington Friends.

A QUAKER GENTLEMAN
WALTER DEW

A QUAKER LADY
EDITH RHOADS

FRIENDS   *Photos by J. Edgar Rhoads*

HISTORICAL PAGEANT

Friends' Meeting, Wilmington

1738-1938

Wilmington Friends School   Wilmington First-Day School

Helen Clark Collins, *General Chairman*

This is the story of Quakers in Wilmington. A story of pioneers, who with patience and care, built up a Meeting. A story of men and women, who through two hundred years have been led by the Inner Light, a deeply spiritual conviction built around George Fox's saying, "There is that of God in every man." Through the "Inner Light" God has spoken directly and they have obeyed His voice. This Light has inspired them to take an active part in education, in social welfare, in prison reform and in peace. During two hundred years they have passed through many crises but ever they have strived to bear testimony to the Christian way of life.

Episode I.

Elizabeth Shipley's Dream and Her Visit to Willingtown, 1735

Place: The Old King's Road from Philadelphia to Maryland crossed the Brandywine Creek at Adams Street, led up the hill, winding around the present Brandywine Cemetery. It was probably about 8th and Franklin Streets that Elizabeth Shipley saw the picture of her dream.

Characters

Elizabeth Shipley—Dorothea Mendinhall; Guide—John M. Mendinhall; Swedish Settler—George A. Morley.

Reader:

In 1725 a ship sailed from Bristol, England, bringing William Shipley and the ancestors of various old families well known in and about Wilmington, including the Tatnalls, Canbys, Leas, Prices, Shipleys, Latimers, Richardsons, and others. William Shipley, together with several other Friends, settled in Ridley, Pennsylvania. Here he married Elizabeth Levis, a gifted member of the Society of Friends. Soon after her marriage, Elizabeth had an impressive dream which has become historic. In the dream Elizabeth saw a beautiful country surrounded by three rivers. It was explained to her that it was the Divine Will that she and her family should settle here and build up a thriving community. The dream was so real and vivid that Elizabeth related it to William, who considered it a flight of fancy. With the many household and business cares it was forgotten, until Elizabeth went on an eventful journey destined to change many lives.

It was in the spring of 1735 that Elizabeth Shipley felt a concern to visit the Meetings in lower Delaware and Maryland. One bright sunny morning she left her family and household cares and set out from her home in Ridley, to journey on horseback along the Old King's Road to Maryland. After traveling through wild unsettled country for six or seven hours, she suddenly came to a stream plunging over rocks between steep wooded banks. The wild current seemed to challenge her to cross, hoarse frogs croaked their warnings. It was a perplexing moment but Elizabeth Shipley was strong in the faith of her mission. Winding her way down the banks she found a fording place. Cautiously she crossed the stream and ascended the long hill before her. With her head bowed in deep meditation she was oblivious to her surroundings until the stumbling of her horse caused her to raise her head. Lo! the picture of her early dream stretched before her. It was all familiar. The rushing creek she had just crossed; in front, the meandering silvery river, the sleepy hamlet by the tidal creek's shore with the great river in the distance on its glistening course to the sea. Her delight merged to a feeling akin to awe at this renewed manifestation of the Divine Will. She no longer doubted. Had not the guide in her dream directed her to this place and commanded that she and her family should be leaders here building up a thriving community?

On her return home, she persuaded her husband, William Shipley, to visit the hamlet of Willingtown. Realizing the rare advantages for both manufacturing and navigation, he purchased land. Because William Shipley was a weighty Friend, many Quakers followed him here.

The Wilmington Meeting of the Society of Friends was established early in the year of 1738.

Dramatization

During the reading Elizabeth Shipley and her guide approach on horseback. They consult briefly with the Swedish settler, then ride off.

At the end of the episode, six people dressed in plain garb enter and take their places on the facing benches at the back of the stage. The men sit on the right-hand side and the women on the left-hand side as was customary in the Wilmington Monthly Meeting.

Episode II.

Scene from the Friends School, 1748-1749

Place: Meeting House on the east side of West Street. This Meeting House was later incorporated in the Friends School Building at 4th and West Streets.

Characters

School Master, Enoch Flowers—James F. Adams, Jr.

Men's Committee: William Shipley—David E. Chambers; David Ferris—James M. Collins; James Lea—Howard W. Starkweather, Jr.

Women's Committee: Dorcas Brown—Marguerite Rhoads; Hannah Jackson—Joann S. Brosius; Jane Reynolds—Rosamond B. Chambers; Rebecca Wood—Elizabeth A. Lahr.

Class I: William—John H. Lowe; John—L. Coleman Dorsey; David—John Richardson; Rachel—Marilyn Dew; Ann—Hester H. Richardson; Orpah—Ann Fletcher.

Class II, Primer Class: Rebecca—Ann W. Shelnutt; Olga—Mary N. Starkweather; Deborah—Mary Lee Jones; Christina—Diantha E. Bartlett; Other Pupils: Thomas R. Dew, Thomas M. Hollingsworth, Henry N. Marsh, Jr., Franklin Taylor, III.

Larger Children: Hannah—Ann Carey; Rest—Margery Metz; Patience—Joyce Silver; Peter—Mark B. Holzman, Jr.; Jonathan—John H. Hollingsworth; Joseph—John M. Vandegrift; Sven—Wills Passmore; Eric—Robert E. Clark, Jr.; Robert—David S. Hollingsworth; Edith—Carolyn A. Schneider.

Reader

The community grew and prospered. A grave concern arose in the Meeting that children have schooling. This resulted in the establishment of Friends School in 1748 in which the Meeting has always taken an active interest. Various members were appointed to oversee the education of not only the children of members, but children in the community whose parents were unable to pay for schooling.

As we see the school this particular 5th month morning, several girls are busy mixing powdered inkberries with water. A few boys are sharpening quills for pens. The teacher is explaining a problem to a larger boy.

Dramatization

Teacher pulls out ponderous watch, goes to door with bell which he rings. Children come in and take their seats.

Rest:—Master Flowers, what shall I do with this ink we have made?

Master Flowers:—Rest, thou mayest place the ink on my desk. 'Tis a goodly quantity.
(Turning to group)
Let us begin our day by repeating the words of David as found in the one hundred twenty-first Psalm.
(Children rise and repeat Psalm. A moment's silence.)

Master Flowers:—Today being the third Fifth Day in the month, we may expect the monthly visit of the School Committee. Let each diligently pursue his own task. Peter, use extreme care in that reduction ascending and descending upon which thou art working. Accurate ciphering will be a help in thy father's business.
(Enter four Women's Committee members—greetings.)

Master Flowers:—Class I in Reading (6 children with Horn Books come forward.)

Master Flowers:—We shall begin with our a, b, c's.

Class and Teacher:—a - b - c - d - e - f, etc.

Master Flowers:—John, thou must keep thy eyes on the letters. Remember "He that ne'er learns his a, b, c's will forever a blockhead be."
Now our syllables—(children repeat after teacher): ba, be, bi, bo, bu; ca, ce, ci, co, cu; da, de, di, do, du.

Master Flowers:—Continue your study when you return to your seats but please do so quietly. I have received complaints from the neighbors that our studying disturbs them.

Master Flowers:—Second Reading Class—(8 children come forward with primers).
Today we shall study words with five syllables.
(Children repeat syllable by syllable, finally saying the word.)

a bo mi na ti on   ed i fi ca ti on
e man ci pa ti on   ge ne ro si ty

Master Flowers:—Very well done; Christina, thou mayest read about the cock.

Christina:—The cock doth crow to let you know
If you be wise, what time to rise.

Master Flowers:—And now about the nightingale, Rebecca and Olga.

Rebecca { The nightingale doth sweetly sing
Olga {   To welcome back the cheerful spring.

Master Flowers:—Boys, read "Duty to God and Our Neighbor."

Boys:—Love God with all our soul and strength
With all our heart and mind;
And love your neighbor as yourself,

Be faithful, just, and kind.
Deal with another as you'd have
Another deal with you.
What you're unwilling to receive
Be sure you never do.

(Enter men of School Committee—greetings.)

Master Flowers:—Is there any subject in which you are particularly interested?

Friend Shipley:—I am much concerned about the poor spelling of this day.

Master Flowers:—Very well, Friend Shipley, I shall call the spelling class. (Nods to children.)

(Eight larger children come forward.)

(Teacher pronounces and children spell in turn. Classes are dismissed for recess.)

(Women take their leave.)

Friend Lea (leaving):—Master Flowers, art thou bearing in mind what farmer Brown said about his son, "The Bible and figgers is all I want my boy to know"?

Master Flowers:—I am, Friend Lea. Good day to you all.

Episode III.

First Day Meeting, 8th Month, 1777

Place: Meeting House Yard, Fourth and West Streets, Seventh Day and First Day Morning.

Characters

Drummer—William G. Simons; Captain—James B. Shelnutt, III; First Soldier—William R. MacIntyre, Jr.; Second Soldier—Harcourt R. Burns, Jr.; Third Soldier—Robert F. Mancill.

Soldiers: Everett M. Aikman, Olin S. Allen, Ernest S. Benger, Samuel Bancroft Bird, Jr., G. William Butz, III, Campbell Cary, Kenneth E. Clarke, George W. K. Forrest, Jr., William Hodgson, Robert B. Johnson, Alan M. Mancill, James T. Mullin, Caleb Johnson Penniman, Cesare A. Protto, Charles W. Stockly, J. David Weiland, Karl A. Williams, Jr.

Committee for Sufferings: James Robinson—Charles G. Shoemaker; Robert Lewis—Edward S. Brinton; Vincent Boncell—Thomas C. Marshall, Jr.; Zechariah Ferris—Thomas M. Wills.

Speaking Friends: Eleanor A. Marshall, Edward S. Brinton, Thomas M. Wills.

Speakers at Meeting: Thomas C. Marshall, Jr., Frances B. Richardson.

Friends Attending Meeting: Joanne Cox, Harriet Lou Frorer, William R. Gawthrop, Jr., Eleanor Glover, Ellen D. Hilles, C. Robert Hollingsworth, Joan I. Hunt, D. Marie Johnston, J. Joseph Kelleher, Jr., Carolyn W. Medill, Maryemma Ryan, Louis M. Sala, Marion Betts Shaw, Florence D. Shelnutt, Elizabeth Silver.

Reader.

During the Revolutionary War, Friends suffered greatly due t their testimony of non-resistance. A committee for Sufferings, as a committee of Advice for all to apply to, was appointed by the Monthly Meeting "to take into consideration the present suffering state of divers Friends belonging to this Meeting."*

On 8th month, 1777, there is an entry in the Records of the Committee: "We are given to understand that Friends' Meeting House in this town is taken up with soldiers, who broke into it yesterday and that (although upon some Friends demanding it to hold meeting in today) some of them promised we should have it by eleven o'clock, yet they did not perform, but kept possession, and Friends held meeting under a shady tree in the grave-yard."

Dramatization

Drums beating, soldiers come marching in.

First Soldier:—Yonder, looks like a good substantial building captain, with plenty of room for all of us. Why not use that for barracks?

Second Soldier:—Ah, I fear it is locked.

Three Soldiers (rush forward):—That's easily remedied. (Banging doors with butts of guns.)

(Soldiers enter. Group singing "Johnny Peel.")

Captain:—Why must you be so rough. Little good comes from such rough usage of a sacred building, no matter what the sect.

(The men make themselves at ease and all quickly assumes an air of disorder.)

(The Committee for Suffering enter, watching proceedings and evidently talking over best procedure.)

Quaker:—May we speak to the leader. (as he steps forward): We are the Committee for Sufferings of this Meeting. We realize your men must have a place to sleep and rest, but we have come to ask that on the First-Day morning we might have the place for our usual hour of worship, eleven o'clock.

Captain:—Gentlemen, I regret the damage already done, but the men are tired and in an ugly mood. However, I give my word that by the morrow I will try to have things tidy and the place ready.

(The speaker shakes his hand and thanks him as they leave.

The soldiers start to drink. Gradually the place becomes very boisterous.)

Reader

On First-day Morning at eleven o'clock, Friends assembled for Meeting, but the soldiers failed to keep their promises made so readily the day before.

Dramatization

Morning: The worshippers begin to gather. They stand to one

---

*From the opening minute of the Records of the Committee for Suffering, 4th month, 1757.

side as they see the state of things.   Three men approach the captain who shakes his head and shrugs as if to say: You see for yourself. What can I do?   The Quaker men join group and discuss what to do.

Quaker:—Never have we needed God's presence and help more direly. Let us convene under yonder tree and worship God beneath it.

(The group gradually becomes quieter and more still till even the children are lost in thought and prayer.)

Message:—Let us remember
"God is our refuge and strength.
A very present help in trouble.
Therefore will not we fear." Ps. 46.

Message:—As I have been sitting here thinking in this unusual Meeting of ours, these words of George Fox have been running through my mind and I should like to share them with the people gathered here today:

"Friends, fear not the Powers of Darkness, but keep your Meetings; and meet in that which keeps you over them; and in the Power of God you shall have Unity."

(After silence, meeting breaks.)

Episode IV.
The Female Benevolent Society, 1800

Scene I.   Organization Meeting, 2nd Mo. 6, 1800, Rebecca Martin Home.

Charter Members: Rebecca Martin—Edna Hart Taylor; Ann White, Jr.— Ann Speakman; Rachel Wood—Margery H. Van Trump; Ann Sipple—Faith Maris; Rachel Hayes, Jr.—Catherine M. Sawyer; Deborah Bringhurst—Janet A. Frorer; Ann Ferris—Ann L. Mason; Gertrude Gilpin—Elizabeth A. Springer; Mary Jones— Frederika H. Bancroft; Mary Canby—Marie Booth; Edith Ferris, Jr.—Mary Louise Shoemaker; Hannah Martin—Alice P. Bradley; Orpah Hewes—Ruthanna Taylor; Ann Spackman—Henrietta Pyle; Fanny Canby—Marion F. Smith; Margaret Canby—Ellen Wood.

Reader

Sixteen young women in the Meeting, who felt a great concern to aid the poor, founded the Female Benevolent Society, the oldest charitable institution in Delaware.   On 2nd month, 6th, 1800, they met at Rebecca Martin's home to consider the constitution and rules of the Society.

Dramatization

The guests arrive in small groups, visiting in low whispers. Rebecca Martin, acting as chairman, opens the meeting.

Photos by J. Edgar Rhoads

PAGEANT 1938

THE LYCEUM   THE FEMALE BENEVOLENT SOCIETY

Rebecca Martin:—We are met here on a matter of great moment. It is not necessary to lay before this group, the purpose of this meeting.

Several of us have met and written a constitution and drawn up some rules which we wish this group to consider. Will someone act as clerk? Thank thee, Deborah.

Deborah (reading):—"A number of young women, who believe, from the observations they have made, that they may render some assistance to their fellow-beings who suffer the afflictions of age, are induced to enter into an association for their relief. As their funds will be inconsiderable they cannot expect to perform Great Works—yet the gift of a Cup of Cold Water, when furnished from a right disposition of mind, has the promise of a blessing annexed to it. Committees shall be appointed to seek and visit without distinction of nation or color, such persons as may be proper objects of their attention and care. Those committees shall endeavor to encourage and promote industry by furnishing employment to such as may be able to work."

Rebecca Martin:—Before the clerk reads the rules, we will consider this constitution. (After a brief pause,) several members—I approve. I approve.

Deborah:—I shall now proceed with the rules:

1. No conversation to be admitted but what relates to the affairs of the Society.

2. It is requested that the hour appointed for Meeting be punctually observed, that the business may be proceeded on without unnecessary delay.

3. Members are desired to arrange domestic affairs so as to attend to the business of the Society in their turn, that each may take an equal share and no individual have too great a burden laid on her.

(After a brief pause)—I approve. I approve.

(Several members at the clerk's suggestion come forward and sign the rules, then all in turn.

After returning to their seats, committees are appointed).

Deborah:—Ann Ferris is appointed treasurer, Ann Sipple assistant clerk. It will be necessary to circulate subscription papers.

Deborah:—It has been suggested that we meet each week on fifth day. Does that meet with the approval of the group?

(After a little discussion, it is approved.)

Deborah:—If there is no further business, the meeting is adjourned to meet at John Ferris' at 6 o'clock P. M. the 13th instant.

(A period of silence, then visiting as the group take their leave.)

Scene II. Store Room, Hemphill House, 5th Mo., 1800

Committee of Work: Edith Ferris, Jr.—Mary Louise Shoemaker; Sally Norris Dickinson—Edna Hart Taylor.

Flax Committee: Hannah Martin—Alice P. Bradley; Ann White—Ann A. Speakman.

Committee of Inspection: Gertrude Gilpin—Elizabeth A. Springer; Ann Sipple—Faith Maris; Mary Canby—Marie Booth; Rachel Hayes, Jr.—Catherine M. Sawyer; Ann Spackman—Henrietta Pyle.

Negro Women: Mary Nicholson—Helen A. Cranston; Lizzy Read—Elizabeth A. Detwiler.

Needy Woman: Lucy Orpon—Ruth Russel Smith.

Physician: Dr. Vaughn—G. Sellers Smith.

Manufacturer: Jacob Broom—Arnold M. Collins.

Member of Board of Health: John Starr—John B. Rhoads.

Clerk: Deborah Bringhurst—Janet A. Frorer.

Reader

The Collection Committee deposited the money it collected with the treasurer. At the request of the Committee of Work, a storeroom, open three afternoons a week, was established in the center of town. Three members were appointed each week to attend it. The group spent many afternoons like this as recorded in the minutes.

Dramatization

(The Committee of Work is looking over the accounts. Ann Spackman enters with a crippled colored woman. Gives her a chair. Consults with Committee. Selects a petticoat and several candles, helps her out while one of the Committee enters the transaction in the book.)

Two white women (entering):—Can we find work here?

S. D.:—Are you good spinners?

Women:—Yes, we are.

S. D.:—Here is a pound of flax. It has been hackled and prepared for spinning. When you return it, I will sort, count and value it. You will be paid in produce according to the market price. (Enters names and amounts in book.)
(Women leave and a colored woman with an order enters. She is given food, material and findings for a dress.)

John Starr (enters):—I took a copy of the Constitution of the Benevolent Society to the Board of Health Meeting last evening. The Board voted to present the Society with six cords of wood which are subject to your order.

Edith Ferris:—That is very kind. The clerk will write a letter thanking the Board.

Dr. Vaughn (stops by):—Gertrude, I have been to see that colored woman, Margaret Larkin. She has consumption. Will you see that she has this medicine? Better take her a warm jacket and some food. (One of the Committee begins to gather up the things preparatory to visiting her.) Just a minute before you go. I will be glad to inoculate for small-pox all the poor children whom you recommend to my care.

Ann Sipple:—I feel sure that a number of parents will be glad to take advantage of your kind offer. I will prepare a list of names and the visitors will tell the parents about it.

(Deborah Bringhurst enters with Jacob Broom. She explains the work, shows him a copy of the constitution and the treasurer's report.)

J. B. (leaving):—Here is ten dollars. (Then as an after-thought as he replaces his wallet)—Let me bid you all a good afternoon. Young ladies, you will hear from me again. I think you are showing good judgment.

Reader

The Female Benevolent Society did hear again from Jacob Broom, a signer of the Constitution of the United States and a member of Old Swedes Church. He left them a legacy with the stipulation that only Members of the Society of Friends could join the Society. The charitable and benevolent work, begun so courageously, by the concerned group of young women in 1800, is still being carried on.

Episode V.

Thomas Garrett Becomes an Abolitionist, About 1813

Scene I. Garrett Farm House, near Upper Darby, Pennsylvania.

Scene II. Near Philadelphia Navy Yard.

Scene III. Near Kensington.

Characters

Mary, the Cook—Anne Glover; Thomas Garrett—Chester Kawel Jones; Sarah Price Garrett—Margaret Davidson.

Kidnappers: John Walker Hoopes, Jr., John Henry Mullin, Jr.

Sailors: John M. Wetherill, James S. Grant, Jr.

Negro Children: Herschel H. Loomis, Jr., W. Rufus Jones, III.

White Children: Mary Lee Jones, L. Coleman Dorsey.

Coachman: Arthur Harmon.

Reader

Friends through their testimony of social justice were deeply concerned about the treatment of the negroes. They took an active part in trying through legislation and abolition societies to abolish slavery. They defended and aided, in every way possible, free negroes who were unlawfully held in bondage. The kidnapping of Thomas Garrett's cook, a free negro, stirred him to become an active abolitionist.

Dramatization

(Mary is sitting in a chair, peeling potatoes into a wooden bowl in her lap and singing a spiritual. The children are playing around her. Two men in a wagon with one loose wheel, which wobbles perceptibly, drive in. They stop wagon, get down, and come up behind Mary and the children, unseen by them. One of the men puts his hand over Mary's mouth, and holds her while the other one tries to catch the children. The children escape.)

Children:—Help! Help! Miz Garrett, help! (The men drag Mary over to the wagon and put her in. As Mrs. Garrett enters, followed timidly by the children, the men whip up the horse and drive off.)

Mrs. Garrett (screaming angrily):—Stop! Stop! Stop! Help! (She sits down in chair and children start to cry in her lap. She tries to comfort them. Hoof-beats are heard and Thomas Garrett rides in. He sees his mother and the children, stops horse, dismounts, and goes over to them.)

Thomas:—Mother, what is troubling thee?

Mrs. Garrett:—Oh, Thomas, Mary's been kidnapped! Two men in a wagon came and took her away. Does thee think we can find her before she is sold?

Thomas (mounting):—Compose thyself, Mother, I'll not come back until I find her. We must put an end to this frightful business. (He gallops off.)

Reader

By following the peculiar tracks which a loose wheel on the wagon made, young Thomas pursued the kidnappers to a place not far from the Navy Yard in Philadelphia. Here he lost the trail in a maze of tracks which covered those of the kidnappers' wagon. The chase seemed almost hopeless, but Thomas was so enraged at the injustice and cruelty of the kidnapping and selling into slavery of a free woman that he was not easily discouraged, and he continued to search for the tell-tale tracks which would show him which way to go.

(Thomas Garrett rides in slowly, watching ground carefully. Some sailors seeing him, call out.)

First Sailor:—Ahoy there! Lose something?

Thomas:—Has thee seen two men in a wagon with a loose wheel?

Second Sailor:—Couple men went by with a wagon load o' straw 'bout half hour ago, askin' the way to Kensington.

Thomas (mounting):—I thank thee kindly. (Gallops off.)

Reader

Thomas was correct in supposing that the men with the load of straw, whom the sailors had seen, were Mary's kidnappers, and some time later he picked up the track of the loose wheel again, on the road to Kensington. Now, sure of his way, Thomas spurred on his horse and the next day overtook the kidnappers.

(Wagon appears with two men sitting in front, Mary sitting behind. Thomas gallops in, passes wagon, turns and heads it off.)

Mary:—Oh, Marse Tom, Lord be praised you're here. (One man turns and hushes Mary, holding her while the other tries to drive past Thomas.)

Thomas:—Let that woman go. Thee can't take her. That woman's free.

First Man:—Git out o' my way afore I run over you.

Second Man:—You can't hold us. We thought she was a runaway. (He lets her go, and she scrambles out of the wagon. Thomas dismounts and goes over to her. The men drive off.)

Mary (slightly hysterical):—Praise de Lawd! Hallelujah! Laws, Marse Tom, Ah shore am glad you got here! Ah was skeered to death dey was gonna sell me. Ah shore am glad to see you.

(They walk off, Thomas leading horse.)

Thomas:—Calm thyself, Mary. Don't thee worry, now. I won't let this happen to thee again. It's time someone did something about these frightful kidnappings.

Episode VI.
Friends Social Lyceum, 1873

Characters

Ellwood Garrett, President—John Welty Wills; Susan Richardson, Secretary— Katherine McKnight; Elizabeth York Case—Ann Cosler; Howard Jenkins—Russell M. Lyman; Ellen Ayers—Jane Bridgewater; Joseph Richardson—Henry Edwin Vinsinger; Laura Webb—Elizabeth I. Adams; Charles Thomas—Herbert H. Ward, III; Henry Ferris—Charles A. Pettit; Emma Worrell—Margaret Sachs; Wilmer Atkinson—Robert Edmond Lincoln; Elizabeth Smith—Mary Callahan; Edith Newlin—Elizabeth Ann Thomas; Margaret Pyle—Jane W. Rayner.

Reader

The younger members of the meeting founded a lyceum to encourage sociability and intellectual growth. During the winter months a meeting was held each second day. The minutes show that the interests of the group were varied and not too serious. This is a meeting as given in the minutes of 1873.

Dramatization

Garrett:—Will you girls please stop giggling so we can begin the meeting? Will the secretary please read the minutes?

Susan (reading):—The Lyceum was called to order at the usual hour by the President. The minutes of the previous meeting were read and approved. No business being presented, the literary exercises were taken up. Emma Worrell read an anonymous article entitled "Pledge with Wine," a forcible argument in favor of total abstinence. Isabel LaSellers followed with a poem by John Greenleaf Whittier, the name of which I didn't catch. Does anyone know what it was?

Ellen Eyre:—"Snowbound", wasn't it?

Susan:—"Snowbound'? I thank thee. (writes). After recess our editress read two excellent articles from "The Sheaf," one of which was an editorial pleading for more contributions, which have been all too scarce of late. Following this came the famous spelling bee between Emma Worrell's and Howard Jenkins' team. (Group bursts out laughing.)

Wilmer:—Girls, quiet down. It's time for the business, spelled b-u-i-s-n-e-s-s, meeting to continue.

Howard (laughing):—That was one time when Emma's star set early.

Emma:—It certainly did. I felt sure that with such a brilliant Swarthmore graduate, my side would win.

Susan (continuing to read):—The meeting was then adjourned.

Respectfully submitted, Susan Richardson, Secretary.

Garrett:—We will start the literary program. Laura Webb will recite John Greenleaf Whittier's "Skipper Ireson's Ride." (Applause).

Now Emma Worrell will read an essay entitled "Inner Selves."*

One of the favorite myths of medieval fairy tales and modern stories of enchantment has been that of some wonderful force by which man might be enabled to spy into the hearts of his fellows either by glasses of miraculous insight conferred on some favored one, or by a force of enchantment, compelling all subjected to certain conditions to speak out the hidden things of the human heart. The moral of such revealment generally appears to be that such revealment is neither profitable nor pleasant, and especially to be dreaded by those compelled to exhibit their inner selves to those around them.

In the old ballad of "True Thomas of Ercildonne" that Dreamer of Huntly Bank is carried away to Fairyland, and has conferred upon him by the Fairy Queen a compulsory gift of perpetual truth-telling which he protests against for reasons whose comic force will appeal to most men. The ballad says:

> "Syne they came on to a garden green
>   And she pu'd an apple frae a tree.
> 'Take this for thy wages, True Thomas,
>   It will give thee the tongue that can never lee.'
>
> 'My tongue is mine ain,' True Thomas he said.
>   ' A gudely gift ye would give to me,
> I neither would dare to buy nor sell
>   At fair or tryst where I may be.'

---

*From a paper written by Emma Worrell, furnished by her niece, Miriam Webb.

'I neither dare to speak to prince nor peer
Nor ask of grace from fair ladye!'
'Now hold thy peace,' the lady said,
'For as I say so must it be'."

Whether this cynical view of the falsehood necessary in the love-making and the bargaining of men still holds good or not, whether we are still shams to greater or less degree is a matter which we may possibly consider, each one for themselves with profit. (Applause).

Garrett:—The meeting is recessed. (All get up and wander out, laughing and talking.)

Episode VII.

The Meeting and First Day School Carry On, 1868-1938

A Quaker Experiment in Friendliness, 1938

Characters

Host—W. Harold Smith, II; Hostess—Caroline Philips.
Dancers:

Swedish Group: Carl Karlsson, Barbara Austin, Margaret Pohl, Greta Karlsson, Carmen Urutia, Yolanda Urutia, Erwin Roberts, Jr., Houston Roberts.

English Group: Jean Broadbent, Dorothy Thomas, Mary Anna Duus, Esther B. Reese, Carolyn W. Medill, Joan Edgar, Jaqueline Russell, Margery Metz, Ann Robinson, Gale Gibson.

American Country Group:—William A. Holmes, Herbert W. Roland, J. Russell Rowland, Jr., William G. Dorsey, Betty Ann Edgar, Christine Dorsey, Helen Broadbent, Madeline Byers, Harriet Lou Frorer, Pauline S. McSparran, Howard J. Hollingsworth, Jr., Donald E. Hollingsworth.

German Group:—Mary Lee Jones, Mary N. Starkweather, Ann Vincent Edgar, Jean Rowland, Louise Duus, Richard K. Sloan, Charles B. Paschall, Joan Paschall, Thomas R. Dew, Diantha E. Bartlett, Frank Taylor, III, Coleman Dorsey, Henry Marsh, Jr.

Procession: Members of First Day School led by Faustina Johnson and J. Russel Rowland, Sr.

Reader

A concern grew in the Meeting that children and young Friends should have instruction in the Bible and Quaker testimonies. T. Clarkson Taylor and Emma Worrell took this concern to the Monthly Meeting and "after obtaining consent of the Monthly Meeting to use the house, this School was opened on First Day afternoon, 1st month, 26, 1868. There was quite a large number of Friends in attendance and about 30, mostly young Friends, volunteered to assist in carrying out the objects of the School. 2 month 2nd, 46 scholars were entered besides 25 or 30 that wished to become both students and teacher."*

The objects of the concerned group have been realized through the large number of young Friends who have gone out from the school. Many have gone far from Wilmington and their influence has been great. They have been among those laboring for peace and mutual understanding among conflicting groups. They have had to make many sacrifices for their convictions. During the World War a number found themselves because of their interpretation of the principles of. Christianity bound to avow that war was utterly incompatible with Christ's teachings. They refused to help in the war and so suffered much through misunderstanding of their attitude toward war. Instead of taking part in the war, they joined with other Friends in the newly organized American Friends Service Committee and helped to "carry on an experiment of love and service by reconstructing many destroyed villages in the war zone of northern France." Some time after the Peace Treaty was signed another group "went to Germany and fed the German children who had been starved by the blockade, and carried on extensive relief and rehabilitation also in Poland."† Since the war, the work of the Service Committee has included not only work for peace throughout the world but also work in our own country for mutual understanding between racial and economic groups. In this work several of our members have had important parts and many have contributed by attending work camps and conferences and all have helped by raising money. They have been pioneers seeking the Christian way of life.

In the past young Friends as well as older ones have had difficult problems to face, but who knows what lies ahead? Here we see an outgrowth of the Quaker experiment in friendliness. It is the evening of the annual party of the International Club in a mining town. The members join in pairs, one American-born woman and one foreign born. Tonight the husbands and children have been invited. It is a gala occasion.

Dramatization

The International Club members come in a few at a time. The foreign born are dressed in native costume. There is much laughter and fooling. The host calls the meeting to order.

---

*From a minute in the original roll book of the F. D. S.
†From a letter to President Roosevelt by Peace Committee of A. F. S. C.

Host:—This is our annual party. We expect everyone to have a good time and also to feel responsible for the other fellow having a good time. Our entertainment this evening is to be a group of dances and a folk song. The first will be a Swedish dance. (Other dances and songs announced in turn.)

Host (after entertainment):—We thank the people who have brought us these dances and songs from their countries. Now it is everyone's turn to become better acquainted. We have made only a start in trying to understand each other's problems. "There will always be suffering, but there will always be young people in search of adventure impelled by curiosity and intellect to find a solution for social problems."*

Two large groups, composed of members of First Day School, Meeting and Friends School enter. Each group leader carries a banner, one with the A. F. S. C. red and black star, the other the Christian flag.

Host:—George Fox said, "I saw that there was an ocean of darkness and death, but I saw also that there was an ocean of light and love which flowed over it." To bring light and love to all requires the devoted effort of every Friend. Led by the Inner Light, let us go forth into service to bring peace and justice to all men. (Silence. Group and audience, led by orchestra and chorus, sing "Hymn of All Nations" by Josephine B. Peabody. Tune: Beethoven's "Hymn of Joy.")

Facing Bench Group: Benjamin K. Smedley, John Richardson, Jr., Edward Bringhurst, W. Ralph Gawthrop, Newlin T. Booth, Leon Spencer, A. Stanley Ayers, Howard J. Hollingsworth, Henry D. Downing, Enos J. Hollingsworth, William C. Philips, John M. Mendinhall, Malcolm A. Brosius, Horace J. Tatnall, Frank S. Garrett, J. Edgar Rhoads, Robert H. Maris, May W. Brosius, Alice P. Sellers, Alice A. Johnson, Margery S. Ayers, Mary S. Malone, Miriam W. Webb, Helen W. Gawthrop, Mary F. Balderston, Janet E. Hallowell, Mary H. Gawthrop, Florence H. Philips, Mary K. Eves, Edith C. Rhoads, Juliet M. C. Pyle, Mary E. Taylor, Estelle Hall Speakman.

Readers: Esther S. Chambers, Walter A. Dew.

Prompter: Ann Walker Bringhurst.

Property Men: James H. Young, Lee Perry.

Pageant Committee, Friends School: Clara G. Dewsnap, Mary B. Passmore, I. Alice Wright, Nancy M. Lyne, George C. Reeser, Susan C. Ingersoll, Sara L. White, Louise A. Wescott. *Friends Meeting:* Helen Collins, general chairman; Evelyn G. Young, Carol Sloan, Faustina Johnson, Ethel Reynolds.

Music, Violins: Carmel De Santis, Joseph Lanzilotti; *Trumpet:* Robert Ingram; *Accordion:* Ellen D. Hilles; *Piano:* Dorothy Broadbent; *Chorus:* Ralph Satterthwaite, leader.

---

*From "Swords Into Plowshares"—Mary Hoxie Jones, 1937.

Brooks Studio

PAGEANT—THE FACING BENCHES

Standing: MARGERY AYERS, MARY EVES, HELEN GAWTHROP, ESTHER | ROBERT MARIS, MALCOLM BROSIUS, JOHN MENDINHALL,
CHAMBERS, MARY BALDERSTON, MARY MALONE, EDITH | FRANK GARRETT, WILLIAM PHILIPS.
RHOADS, ALICE SELLERS.
Seated: FLORENCE PHILIPS, MIRIAM WEBB, MARY GAWTHROP, MAY | BENJAMIN SMEDLEY, JOHN RICHARDSON, EDWARD BRINGHURST,
BROSIUS, ALICE SPACKMAN, ALICE JOHNSON. | RALPH GAWTHROP, NEWLIN BOOTH.

THE ROLL CALL

Carolien Chambers Philips

When the mists have risen above us,
  As our Father knows His own,
Face to face with those who love us,
  We shall know as we are known.
Low beyond the orient meadows,
  Floats the golden fringe of day;
Heart to heart we'll bide the shadows,
  Till the mists have rolled away.

Annie Herbert

	Died
Ella F. G. Baily	4-*-1928
James Baily	7- 1-1909
Jesse W. Baily	8-13-1907
Joseph H. Baily	7-13-1902
Lloyd Balderston	6- 4-1933

Minister, Teacher, Adviser.
Staunch advocate of personal righteousness and of justice for all races.

Emma C. Bancroft	2-15-1929

Overseer, member of Ministry and Counsel. Valued member of Friends' School Committee.

Integrity and Sincerity were qualities which took living form in her life, giving her personality great power and strength.

Henry Bancroft	1-12-1911
Joseph Bancroft	5- 6-1936
Mary R. Bancroft	12- 4-1933
Samuel Bancroft, Jr.	4-22-1915
William P. Bancroft	4-20-1928

Clerk, Overseer, Trustee, Member of Ministry and Counsel, Valued member of Friend's School Board.

A good citizen of a singular modesty and sincerity. His utmost thought of himself might have been expressed: "I pray thee then, write me as one who loved his fellowmen."

	Died
Martha H. Barton	9-24-1933
Aseneth Bartram	4- *-1911
Elizabeth R. Beatty	9-26-1928
Joseph A. Bond	5-23-1907
Dorothy Booker	11-27-1925
Homer W. Booker	11-17-1933
Lydia T. Booker	1-14-1916
Waddington Bradway	1-10-1905
Edward Bringhurst, Jr.	4-23-1912

Trustee.

Elizabeth Bringhurst	1- 7-1922
Esther W. Bringhurst	7- 5-1911
Hannah H. Bringhurst	10-14-1904
Margaret R. Bringhurst	7- 5-1923
Mary W. Bringhurst	11-11-1911
Mary Bringhurst	2- 2-1916
Sarah R. Bringhurst	11-11-1910
Lewis W. Brosius	10- 9-1930

Elder, Member of Ministry and Counsel, and School Board; Assistant Clerk.
Deeply interested in prison reform and temperance.

William R. Bullock	11-18-1914
Elizabeth E. Bullock	1-16-1907
Mary E. Bullock	1-15-1909

	Died
Samuel Bunting	5-29-1906
Phoebe P. Bye	1- 4-1903
Eva B. Cassidy	10-12-1936
Amy L. Chambers	6-26-1903
David B. Chambers	12-21-1906
George W. Chambers	9-25-1916
Mary R. Chambers	8- 8-1926
Elizabeth S. Chandler	1-31-1923
Philemma Chandler	8-19-1918
Rebecca P. Churchman	2-23-1936
Helen E. Clarkson	3-20-1929
Sara B. Clarkson	1-24-1936
Hannah I. K. Clement	8- 6-1924
John F. Comly	7-25-1907
Richard S. Conard	6- 4-1900
Robert H. Conly	*- *-1930
Lydia E. Cox	2- 5-1914
Edwin J. Cranston	11-26-1930
John A. Cranston	10-21-1935

Trustee, Elder, Ministry and Counsel. A devoted member of Meeting.
A supporter of all worthy causes, both civic and charitable.

Martha L. Cranston	6-23-1927

Elder, Ministry, and Counsel.
An ardent worker in the W. C. T. U. and for the enfranchisement of women.

William B. Cranston	*- *-1934
Caroline M. Crismore	4-15-1911
Hannah E. Davis	9- 3-1911
Mary S. P. Derrickson	6-11-1920
Margaret E. Dixon	3-28-1907
Margaret W. Dixon	7-14-1905
Edward B. Downing	3-10-1930
Frances F. Downing	11-19-1935

Overseer, School Board.
Deeply interested in the activities of the Meeting.

Joseph M. Downing	4- 4-1915
Amos A. Eastburn	5-16-1917
Sarah S. England	10- 7-1918

	Died
Albert L. Entriken	1- 3-1917
H. Ida K. Evans	12-29-1932

Overseer.
Deeply interested in Philanthropic work.

John Evans	5-21-1927
Elizabeth Faron	12-12-1920
Ezra Fell	6-12-1910
Marietta Fell	4- 1-1913
Philena Fell	2- 4-1909

Overseer, Ministry and Counsel.

R. Elizabeth Fell	1- 6-1917
Samuel L. Fell	11-27-1914
Sara M. Fell	3- 7-1911

Ministry and Counsel.

Benjamin Ferris	2- 5-1929
David Ferris	4-20-1908

Overseer, Ministry and Counsel.

Martha Ferris	6- 6-1912
Mary W. Ferris	9-26-1907
Matilda Ferris	2-12-1937

Ministry and Counsel, and School Board.
A devoted member of the Meeting. Her loving, cheerful spirit was shown in her frequent messages in the religious meetings and her constant search for truth was an inspiration.

William Canby Ferris	6- 7-1928
William Ferris	1-25-1909
Ann Catherine Flinn	1-24-1901
Ann Fothergill	3- 1-1918
Margaret Fothergill	3-13-1919
Henry Forsythe	8- 9-1924
Catharine Frist	12- 2-1936
Mary Ann Fulton	4-19-1902
Catherine Ann Garrett	8- 4-1900
Elwood Garrett	5-25-1910

School Board.

Henry Garrett	*- *-1903
Henry Garrett, Jr.	7-17-1931
Howard Garrett	6- 1-1928
Maurice Garrett	10- *-1928

	Died		Died
Warren Garrett	5- 1-1920	Sarah E. Johnson	10-26-1908
William R. Garrett	1- 6-1928	S. Marshall Johnson	7- *-1920
Edith M. Gause	5-23-1914	Trustee.	
Allen Gawthrop, Jr.	8- 4-1919	Ann J. Jones	6-27-1915
J. Newlin Gawthrop	4-12-1916	Anna G. Kent	12-14-1901
Overseer, Trustee, School Board.		Daniel H. Kent	12-21-1901
Rebecca A. Gawthrop	2- 7-1929	Lindley C. Kent	2-12-1916
Elder, Overseer, School Board, Ministry and Counsel.		Overseer.	
Richard P. Gibbons	4- 3-1904	Sarah E. Kimmey	3- 9-1913
Ann Good	6-27-1906	Eliza M. Kinnard	2-24-1937
Mary A. Gray	5- 7-1923	Sarah Ann Kirk	2-21-1915
Amanda Grier	12-29-1925	John H. Klund	11- 9-1920
Mary Hackett	5- 6-1917	Enos Larkin	12- 2-1918
Alfred A. M. Hallman	9-25-1928	Mary W. Lindley	11-26-1927
Mary J. Hallman	12-11-1916	Samuel E. Lloyd	4-16-1912
Martha F. Hanna	9- 6-1905	Mary D. Malone	7-18-1931
E. Anne Hannum	9-30-1923	Anna Mary Mansell	1-14-1910
Alice F. Hatton	2-20-1904	Anna H. Maris	5-14-1937
Edwin W. Heald	10- *-1932	Deborah D. Maris	10-18-1937
Elsie R. Heald	11-22-1912	Overseer whose interest in her flock kept their birthdays in mind to the end of her long life.	
Hannah P. Heald	12-10-1908		
Laura S. Heald	12-28-1927	Katharine S. Maris	1-13-1936
Pusey Heald	8- 1-1928	Rebecca D. Maris	3-31-1925
Emlen Hewes	8-25-1907	An Elder, but remembered by her pupils as a kindly teacher of Wilmington School and Governess at Westtown.	
David M. Hillegas	3-19-1935		
Overseer, Trustee.			
Elizabeth B. Hilles	7- 1-1907	Richard Maris	12-29-1934
Margaret S. Hilles	12-31-1912	Trustee of the Meeting for many years.	
Sarah T. Hilles	3-12-1915	Comly M. Marshall	11-21-1922
Willis S. Holden	8- 5-1914	Hannah J. Martin	6- 7-1923
Overseer, Trustee.		Interested in Philanthropic Work.	
Emily P. M.		Jesse W. Martin	6- 6-1927
Hollingsworth	5- 5-1929	Enoch P. H. Martin	12- 9-1905
Dillwyn Hoopes	10- 3-1911	John B. Martin	2-20-1924
James G. Hoopes	2-17-1904	Frances A. Mather	4-27-1904
Mary J. Hoopes	10-17-1933	ElizabethN.McAllister	11-28-1920
Teacher in Friends School.		Overseer.	
Phoebe J. Hoopes	11-10-1927	Mary J. McCullough	1-31-1929
William W. Hoopes	3- 4-1909	Mary C. McDaniel	11- 5-1903

	Died		Died
Janet L. McSparran	11- 8-1930	Samuel D. Paschall	2-19-1916
Edward Mendinhall	8-10-1913	Henry Passmore	5-22-1931
Trustee.		Thomas H. Passmore	12-10-1919
Lydia S. Mendinhall	4-26-1920	Wills Passmore	8- 8-1912
Milton Mendinhall	9- 9-1908	Ministry and Counsel.	
Eva Chambers Miller	*- *-1923	Mary A. Peirson	8- 8-1932
George B. Miller	2-22-1935	Mary G. Pennington	6-23-1927

George B. Miller — Clerk, Assistant Clerk, School Board. Deeply interested in education and in the promotion of music in the First-day School. A pillar of strength in the meeting and in the community.

	Died		Died
		Rebecca M. Pennock	2-26-1914
		Albina Philips	12-27-1916
		Bertha Philips	5- 5-1921
		Hannah J. Philips	11-11-1909
Mary G. Miller	12-31-1936	Harriet C. Philips	2-20-1919
		Helen H. Philips	9-10-1933

Mary G. Miller — Clerk, Assistant Clerk, Trustee, Treasurer of Friend's School—serving with great distinction.

Helen H. Philips — Overseer, Clerk, Assistant Clerk, Secretary of Friends School Board for more than twenty-five years.

	Died		Died
Walter D. Mode	2-29-1928	James Watson Philips	3-31-1936
Helen T. Morse	6- *-1921	John C. Philips	5-22-1922
Emmarine T. Naylor	4-17-1909	Overseer.	
Elizabeth F. Newlin	12-13-1931		

John C. Philips — Most faithful in attendance at Meeting and in supporting its activities.

Elizabeth F. Newlin — Ministry and Counsel. A most acceptable and loving Minister.

	Died		Died
Frances Newlin	2- 8-1906	John Cooper Philips	1-12-1919
Gertrude W. Nields	9- 7-1929	Martha C. Philips	6-30-1922
Herschel A. Norris	3-10-1923	Ellen Pierson	4-27-1936
		George W. Pierson	9- *-1930
		Richard P. Pim	4-30-1924
		William Poole	1-17-1918

Herschel A. Norris — Principal of Friends School from 1898-1922.

William Poole — Clerk, Treasurer, Ministry and Counsel, School Board.

	Died		Died
Caroline Oakford	1-31-1925	William V. Press	6- 3-1925
Ministry and Counsel.		Frederic L. Pyle	5-11-1931
Emma Oakford	4- 4-1900	Assistant Clerk.	
Edward C. Painter	6- 5-1910	Mary B. Pyle	12- 4-1904
Emilie W. Palmer	8- 3-1932	Overseer, School Board.	
Henry W. Palmer	10-25-1908	Orphia C. Pyle	12-23-1924
Wilmer Palmer	8-17-1917	Elizabeth Pusey	12- 2-1909
Trustee.		Fanny M. Pusey	12-27-1915
Franklin Pancoast	* -*-1901	Jane R. Pusey	12-31-1918
Charles Paschall	7-18-1909	Jonas Pusey	2- 4-1910
John Paschall	12- 9-1926	Eleanore D. Reed	12- 3-1912
Franklin Paschall	4-15-1908	Margaret C. Reeves	12-15-1912
Katherine Paschall	4-10-1936		
Henry H. Paschall	7-18-1909		

Died

Alice M. K. Reid   11- 1-1922

Lydia Reynolds   4-26-1922

David J. Reinhardt   11-22-1935
Teacher in Friends School. Well known Attorney for many years and a Judge in the Delaware Courts.

Joseph Reinhardt   7-14-1906

John S. Reinhart   5- 5-1932

Mary S. Rinehart   11- 1-1905

Frances G. Rhoads   1-14-1903

Frances Tatum Rhoads 8-26-1931
A loving Minister.

George A. Rhoads   5- 8-1937
Clerk, Overseer, Elder. Devoted to the interests of the Meeting.

John Tatum Rhoads   7-30-1907

Jonathan E. Rhoads   9-14-1914
A Minister who lived his favorite text: Seek ye first the Kingdom of God.

Rebecca G. Rhoads   4-16-1905
Clerk, Overseer, Elder.

Alice A. Richardson   9-16-1922

Anna B. Richardson   11- 5-1904

John Richardson   6- 2-1904

MargaretR. Richardson 3-29-1900

Mary A. Richardson   9-28-1911

Martha Richardson   10-17-1923

Martha A. Richardson   5- 6-1918

James V. Roberts   10-30-1931
An earnest friend whose kindly, cheerful, spirit still lives.

Louise Roberts   12- *-1935

Julian B. Robinson   7-20-1936

Rachel A. Robinson   5-27-1900

Sarah M. Robinson   7-21-1936
Long remembered for her perennial optimism and her most faithful attendance at Meeting, always welcoming the visitors. Especially interested in young people and in all the activities of the Meeting.

Lucy H. Satterthwait 12- *-1924

Died

Margaret S.
    Satterthwaite   8-13-1912

Reuben Satterthwaite   5-10-1922

Emeline P. Seal   2-28-1926

William A. Seal   12-21-1919

Anne W. Sellers   8-27-1912

Frances G. Sellers   4-23-1925

Joshua K. Sharpless   6-25-1917

Fred T. Sheward   1-28-1911

Rachel A. Sheward   8- 2-1928

StephenC.Singleton III 1-12-1919

Beatrice S. Sisley   4-11-1931

Arthur C. Smedley   9-28-1918

M. Esther Smedley   4-20-1921

Rowena B. Smedley   2-26-1910

Albert W. Smith   3- 2-1914
    Overseer, School Board.

Arthur H. Smith   10-13-1905

Charles W. Smith   1-23-1936

Dewees Smith   8-26-1904

Isabell Sellers Smith   1-30-1935

Linton Smith   10-20-1927
    Trustee.

W. Harold Smith   2-23-1936

Clement B. Smyth   7-11-1901

Sarah Sellers Smyth   5-20-1911

George H. Spackman   2-13-1920

Allen Speakman   10-21-1905

Anna A. Speakman   5-11-1933

Samuel Speakman   9- 5-1910

Willard A. Speakman   6-24-1936

R. Barclay Spicer   7-12-1924

Emma A. Stapler   9- 4-1932

Lydia S. Suplee   1-16-1927

Mary H. Tanguy   3- 7-1910

William S. Tanguy   3- 9-1921

Edward Tatnall   5-25-1914

Joseph R. Tatnall   5-10-1910

Lucy R. Tatnall   10-23-1936
    Elder.

	Died
Rachel A. Tatnall	10-18-1927
Clerk, Overseer, Elder, worker.	
John R. Tatum	8- 7-1902
Elder of great understanding.	
Lucy R. Tatum	2-26-1908
Elder.	
Elizabeth M. Taylor	3-28-1903
Overseer.	
Franklin Taylor	9-17-1911
H. Clayton Taylor	7-17-1906
Henry M. Taylor	1-14-1918
Lydia F. Taylor	3-16-1904
Marietta S. Taylor	1-14-1933
Mary E. Thomas	4-29-1927
Phoebe T. Thomas	1-24-1923
Ruth Ann Thomas	3-13-1920
Albina P. Thompson	10-22-1929
George R. Thompson	7-19-1924
Principal of Friends School.	
Hannah M. Thompson,	2- 5-1922
Elder, Ministry and Counsel.	
Elizabeth S. Thorp	4- 8-1925
Howard J. Thorp	12-30-1925
Margaret S. Thorp	10-26-1906
Thomas Thorp	2- 2-1902
Charles N. Trump	12-30-1912
Trustee.	
Helen M. Trump	9-17-1910
Juliet Canby Trump	3- 4-1928
Rosamond C. Trump	6-17-1927
Samuel N. Trump	10- 6-1916
Charles R. VanTrump	11- 2-1924
Howell H. VanTrump	5-19-1904
William C. VanTrump	2-20-1926
Elsie Janney Walter	10-11-1921
Granville W. Walter	8-20-1902
Naomi R. Walter	10-19-1912

	Died
Alfred D. Warner	12- 6-1915
Trustee.	
Eliza J. Watson	4-10-1902
Herbert K. Watson	5- 4-1936
Joseph W. H. Watson	9-25-1900
Martha Watson	9-29-1929
School Board, Ministry and Counsel.	
Alfred H. Way	7- 5-1917
Chandler R. Way	12- *-1902
Charles C. Way	9-15-1924
Henry R. Way	10-13-1910
Josephine H. Way	5-25-1903
L. Anna Way	4- 7-1936
Anna Webb	3-24-1906
Laura Worrell Webb	1-14-1934
Treasurer of Female Benevolent Society, Friends School Board.	
William P. Webb	6-20-1911
Overseer, worker in Firstday School.	
Edward S. West	4-31-1906
Mary E. Williams	5-12-1927
Mary Wilson	9-21-1910
Rachel Wilson	4-30-1905
Ministry and Counsel.	
Mary S. Woodward	11-18-1912
Franklin Wooley	3- 1-1907
Emma Worrell	11-12-1930
Elder, Overseer, Ministry and Counsel. A distinguished teacher. Worker for the enfranchisement of women. Keen sympathy and understanding.	
Granville Worrell	12-11-1910
Miriam C. Worrell	8-20-1905
Thomas Worrell	7-17-1904
Charlotte Ann Yarnall	4-19-1921
James Weston Yarnall	2- 5-1914
Phoebe A. Yarnall	4-19-1921

QUAKER WEDDINGS

Mary B. Passmore

RIENDS have always considerd marriage as being a religious act and a covenant between two people. Hence they have adopted a procedure that requires no additional person in the ceremony.

The marriage is accomplished in a religious meeting of Friends and relatives and may be celebrated at a private home, though earlier it was usual to have the couple appear in a "public meeting of the Religious Society of Friends."

Permission from the Monthly Meeting must be obtained by the participants and a Committee of Oversight appointed to see that the requirements of the laws are fulfilled and that fitting simplicity be observed in the marriage procedure. Up to 1807 the records state that permission was asked of "the several Monthly Meetings of the people called Quakers".

In the following record the weddings are listed chronologically. If held in one of the Wilmington Meeting houses, such is indicated by:[1] Second Meeting House, Fourth and West Streets;[2] present Meeting House, Fourth and West Streets;[3] Meeting House, Ninth and Tatnall Streets;[4] Meeting House, Tenth and Harrison Streets. If not so marked, the wedding was at a meeting outside Wilmington or at a private home.

Robert Richardson and Sarah Shipley[1]	10th mo. 6th, 1750
Henry Troth and Sarah Paschall[1]	2nd mo. 25th, 1751
William Evans and Catharine Wollaston	9th mo. 19th, 1751
Joseph Hewes and Rachel Bell[1]	4th mo. 16th, 1752
William Morris and Rebekah Peters[1]	10th mo. 5th, 1752
Thomas Canby and Elizabeth Lewis[1]	7th mo. 26th, 1753
William Shipley and Sarah Rumford[1]	12th mo. 27th, 1753
Samuel Wharton and Sarah Lewis	2nd mo. 15th, 1754
Daniel Jackson and Ann Warner[1]	5th mo. 23rd, 1754
William Poole and Martha Roberts[1]	6th mo. 27th, 1754
Thomas Underhill and Rachel Mendinhall[1]	7th mo. 25th, 1754
William Warner and Sarah Eldridge[1]	10th mo. 31st, 1754
John Clempson and Elizabeth Way[1]	1st mo. 10th, 1755
William Dean and Katherine King[1]	1st mo. 16th, 1755

John Stuart and Hannah Lea[1]	6th mo. 10th, 1756
Henry Drinker and Ann Swett	3rd mo. 4th, 1757
Thomas Gilpin and Ann Caudwell[1]	5th mo. 19th, 1757
William Marshall and Mary Tatnall[1]	8th mo. 25th, 1757
John Hobson and Elizabeth Warner[1]	9th mo. 29th, 1757
Gouldsmith Folwell and Sarah Cadwalader[1]	5th mo. 31st, 1759
Bancroft Woodcock and Ruth Andrews[1]	6th mo. 28th, 1759
Thomas Parry and Catherine Dean[1]	5th mo. 29th, 1760
Aaron Ashbridge and Mary Tomlinson	6th mo. 4th, 1760
William White and Ann McMullen[1]	8th mo. 21st, 1760
Job Harvey and Sarah Dawes[1]	10th mo. 30th, 1760
Benjamin Canby and Susannah Littler[1]	12th mo. 25th, 1760
William Woodcock and Elizabeth Marshall[1]	1st mo. 22nd, 1761
Benjamin Yarnall and Elizabeth Folwell[1]	4th mo. 30th, 1761
Ezekiel Andrews and Rebekah Robinson[1]	5th mo. 28th, 1761
William Poole and Elizabeth Canby[1]	12th mo. 3rd, 1761
Thomas Lamborn and Dinah Carsan[1]	4th mo. 1st, 1762
Robert Johnson and Mary Wolaston[1]	6th mo. 3rd, 1762
William Troth and Lydia Osborne[1]	8th mo. 4th, 1763
John Andrews and Sarah Ferriss[1]	8th mo. 25th, 1763
John Littler and Sarah Stapler[1]	10th mo. 27th, 1763
Philip Jones and Edith Newlin[1]	5th mo. 31st, 1764
William Jenkins and Hannah Littler[1]	6th mo. 28th, 1764
Jeremiah Carter and Rebekah Wiley[1]	12th mo. 27th, 1764
Joseph Tatnall and Elizabeth Lea[1]	1st mo. 31st, 1765
Richard Richardson and Sarah Tatnall[1]	4th mo. 24th, 1766
Hezekiah Niles and Mary Way[1]	7th mo. 17th, 1766
William Lightfoot and Mary Ferriss[1]	8th mo. 14th, 1766
Richard Dickinson and Phebe Carsan[1]	10th mo. 16th, 1766
Phineas Buckley and Mary Shipley[1]	5th mo. 12th, 1768
William Ashburnham and Rosanna Ferriss[1]	5th mo. 19th, 1768
Jonathan Woodnutt and Betty Wilson[1]	9th mo. 15th, 1768
Edward Wells and Sarah Littler[1]	4th mo. 27th, 1769
James Kightley and Elizabeth Wood[1]	10th mo. 19th, 1769
William Wollaston and Elizabeth England[1]	10th mo. 4th, 1770
Joseph Townsend and Hannah Ferriss[1]	10th mo. 25th, 1770
John Elliott and Margaret Harvey[1]	4th mo. 4th, 1771
Joseph Canby and Hannah Lea[1]	10th mo. 22nd, 1772
John Hill and Ann Hunt[1]	6th mo. 17th, 1773
James Marshall and Margaret Lea[1]	11th mo. 25th, 1773
John Yarnall and Elizabeth Newlin[1]	2nd mo. 3rd, 1774
Thomas Shipley and Rebekah Andrews[1]	4th mo. 27th, 1775
Samuel Canby and Frances Lea[1]	6th mo. 29th, 1775
Joseph Coleman and Sarah Minshall[1]	9th mo. 14th, 1775
George Carsan and Lydia James[1]	12th mo. 14th, 1775
James Berry and Mary Bonsall[1]	2nd mo. 15th, 1776
William Zane and Ann Bennett[1]	5th mo. 16th, 1776

George Martin and Elizabeth Reynolds[1]	11th mo. 28th, 1776
Charles Wharton and Elizabeth Richardson[1]	10th mo. 22nd, 1778
Thomas Bryan and Ann Kells[1]	4th mo. 15th, 1779
William Goodwin and Elizabeth Brown[1]	11th mo, 11th, 1779
John Webster and Lydia Mendinghall[1]	4th mo. 13th, 1780
James Pierce, Jr. and Miriam Carsan[1]	5th mo. 11th, 1780
Thomas Newlin and Sarah Berry[1]	11th mo. 16th, 1780
Gerard Blackford and Sarah Price[1]	7th mo. 12th, 1781
Griffith Minshall and Mercy Dawes[1]	12th mo, 13th, 1781
Thomas Marriott and Mary Sheward[1]	5th mo. 30th, 1782
John Underhill and Elizabeth Johnson[1]	10th mo. 30th, 1782
Joseph Price and Rosanna Ashburnham[1]	6th mo. 12th, 1783
Henry Troth and Hannah Starr[1]	9th mo. 18th, 1783
John Ferriss and Ann Gilpin[1]	9th mo. 25th, 1783
Eliakim Garretson and Lydia Windle[1]	11th mo. 27th, 1783
James Reynolds and Hannah Webster[1]	5th mo. 20th, 1784
William Byrnes and Anna Shipley[1]	10th mo. 28th, 1784
Joshua Stroud and Martha Byrnes	1st mo. 19th, 1785
Thomas Lea and Sarah Tatnall[1]	1st mo. 20th, 1785
John Stapler and Jemima Robinson[1]	6th mo. 16th, 1785
James Robinson and Betty Wilson[1]	7th mo. 21st, 1785
Isaac Jackson and Elizabeth Rea[1]	11th mo. 17th, 1785
Samuel Nichols and Ruth Mendinghall[1]	12th mo. 15th, 1785
Nathaniel Richards and Lydia Pritchett[1]	12th mo. 29th, 1785
John Commons and Sarah Wollaston	11th mo. 22nd, 1786
John Kendall and Mary Gibbons[1]	4th mo. 26th, 1787
Thomas Robinson and Mary Wilson[1]	10th mo. 5th, 1787
Thomas Wickersham and Sarah Johnson	10th mo. 11th, 1787
John James and Rachel Woodcock[1]	10th mo. 11th, 1787
Eli Mendinghall and Phebe Pritchett[1]	10th mo. 18th, 1787
Caleb Seal and Alice Clark[1]	11th mo. 22nd, 1787
John Poles Seal and Mary Jackson	9th mo. 17th, 1788
Solomon Phillips and Martha Nichols	10th mo. 22nd, 1788
Joseph Wilkinson and Margaret Starr[1]	11th mo. 13th, 1788
William Richards and Catharine Phillips	11th mo. 19th, 1788
Ellis Sanders and Edith Yarnall	4th mo. 1st, 1789
Gerard Blackford and Elizabeth Serrell[1]	4th mo. 30th, 1789
Richard Jacobs and Phebe Eaves	7th mo. 30th, 1789
Vincent Bonsall and Mary Askew[1]	9th mo. 24th, 1789
Thomas Shallcross and Deborah Claypoole Potts[1]	10th mo. 22nd, 1789
Samuel Stroud and Elizabeth Richardson[1]	10th mo. 29th, 1789
Abraham Gibbons and Mary Canby[1]	5th mo. 27th, 1790
Cyrus Newlin and Sarah Shipley[1]	6th mo. 24th, 1790
John Johnson and Hannah Sheward[1]	10th mo. 7th, 1790
John White and Mary Robinson[1]	10th mo. 21st, 1790
Abraham Bonsall and Mary Andrews[1]	10th mo. 28th, 1790
Joseph Bailey and Elizabeth Tatnall[1]	11th mo. 25th, 1790
Henry Reynolds and Mary Kendall[1]	6th mo. 30th, 1791

Joseph Thomas and Elizabeth Chambers	10th mo. 19th, 1791
John Elliot and Sarah Johnson	10th mo. 26th, 1791
James Gilpin and Sarah Littler[1]	4th mo. 26th, 1792
Timothy Hanson and Mary Robinson[1]	5th mo. 17th, 1792
John Jones and Ann Shipley[1]	9th mo. 20th, 1792
Richard Barnard and Sarah Chambers	10th mo. 24th, 1792
Samuel Coope and Elizabeth Blackford[1]	10th mo. 25th, 1792
Robert Leslie and Rachel Rogers	3rd mo. 20th, 1793
Isaac Starr and Margaret Tatnall[1]	12th mo. 26th, 1793
William Elliott and Esther Griffith[1]	5th mo. 22nd, 1794
David Chandler and Miriam Peirce[1]	6th mo. 12th, 1794
Jesse Shenton Zane and Susannah Hanson[1]	9th mo. 18th, 1794
Thomas Sipple and Ann Tatnall[1]	9th mo. 25th, 1794
Thomas Downing and Mary Spackman[1]	12th mo. 25th, 1794
Robert Squibb and Mary Hamilton[1]	5th mo. 21st, 1795
John Biddle and Elizabeth Canby[1]	9th mo. 15th, 1796
William Dixon Phillips and Phebe Starr[1]	10th mo. 20th, 1796
Reuben Haines and Mary Johnson	4th mo. 19th, 1797
William Warner and Esther Tatnall[1]	4th mo. 19th, 1798
William Robinson and Elizabeth Hanson[1]	5th mo. 24th, 1798
Charles Green and Hannah Squibb[1]	11th mo. 15th, 1798
Thomas Squibb and Rachel Foster[1]	5th mo. 16th, 1799
Joseph Bringhurst, Jr. and Deborah Ferriss[1]	7th mo. 11th, 1799
Isaac Baily and Sarah Yarnall	8th mo. 22nd, 1799
John Ferriss, Jr. and Sarah Harlan	10th mo. 22nd, 1800
John Dixon and Mary Shipley[1]	4th mo. 15th, 1802
Joseph Grubb and Hester Spackman[1]	4th mo. 22nd, 1802
Warner Rasin and Margaret Wilkinson[1]	11th mo. 11th, 1802
John Erwin and Elizabeth Platt[1]	11th mo. 18th, 1802
Jonathan Evans and Elizabeth Pedrick[1]	2nd mo. 17th, 1803
Robert Wilkinson and Rachel Wood[1]	5th mo. 12th, 1803
Joseph Richardson and Ann Spackman[1]	6th mo. 16th, 1803
Christopher Hollingsworth, Jr. and Elizabeth Horner[1]	7th mo. 14th, 1803
Daniel McPherson and Elizabeth Grubb[1]	10th mo. 6th, 1803
William Paxson and Ann Canby[1]	10th mo. 20th, 1803
Caleb Harlan, Jr. and Edith Ferriss, Jr.[1]	12th mo. 22nd, 1803
Benjamin Ferris and Fanny Canby[1]	5th mo. 17th, 1804
Eli Mendinhall and Mary Wayne[1]	10th mo. 11th, 1804
William Walker and Jane Sheward[1]	10th mo. 17th, 1805
Horton Howard and Hannah Hastings[1]	12th mo. 5th, 1806
Jeremiah Wollaston and Mary Chambers	1st mo. 14th, 1807
Joshua Johnson and Margaret Carty	5th mo. 13th, 1807
Isaac Whitelock and Ann Marot[1]	5th mo. 14th, 1807
John Morton, Jr. and Margaret Canby[1]	2nd mo. 18th, 1808
Albanus Charles Logan and Maria Dickinson[1]	4th mo. 28th, 1808
Peter Mason and Martha Way[1]	4th mo. 13th, 1809
James Brian and Mary Hastings[1]	4th mo. 20th, 1809
Edward Tatnall and Margery Paxson[1]	10th mo. 12th, 1809

Clement Biddle and Mary Canby[1]	11th mo. 22nd, 1810
Joseph Hance and Martha Pyle	12th mo. 13th, 1810
Caleb Stroud and Esther Stapler	1st mo. 23rd, 1811
Barrett Mason and Ann Williamson[1]	4th mo. 11th, 1811
John Hewes and Mary Megear[1]	6th mo. 20th, 1811
Peter Askew and Hannah Wilkinson[1]	10th mo. 17th, 1811
Asa Moore and Ann Littler[1]	10th mo. 24th, 1811
Daniel Dawson and Sarah Stapler	4th mo. 15th, 1812
John Stapler and Ann Brian[1]	5th mo. 14th, 1812
Josiah F. Clement and Esther Canby[1]	5th mo. 6th, 1813
John Richardson and Margaret Paxson[1]	5th mo. 13th, 1813
Samuel Malin and Susannah P. Harvey[1]	9th mo. 16th, 1813
Jacob Pusey and Hannah Nichols[1]	11th mo. 4th, 1813
John W. Sherwood and Elizabeth Askew[1]	12th mo. 8th, 1814
Evan Lewis and Sidney Ann Gilpin[1]	3rd mo. 9th, 1815
David Smyth and Anna Canby[1]	10th mo. 12th, 1815
Thomas Rudolph and Hannah Powel[1]	3rd mo. 7th, 1816
Daniel Byrnes and Esther Fussel[1]	5th mo. 9th, 1816
Ziba Ferris and Eliza Megear[1]	11th mo. 14th, 1816
John Sellers, Jr. and Elizabeth Poole[1]	4th mo. 10th, 1817
Reuben Webb and Sarah Jones[1]	5th mo. 8th, 1817
Jacob Pusey and Hannah Mendenhall[2]	5th mo. 7th, 1818
George Robinson and Elizabeth Barker[2]	10th mo. 8th, 1818
Mahlon Betts and Mary Seal[2]	10th mo. 8th, 1818
James R. Squibb and Catharine H. Bonsall[2]	10th mo. 15th, 1818
Jonathan Lamborn and Martha Squibb[2]	11th mo. 5th, 1818
Aaron Hewes and Hannah Commons[2]	4th mo. 8th, 1819
Stephen Bonsall and Mary Stroud[2]	4th mo. 15th, 1819
Stephen Pancoast and Ann Stroud[2]	11th mo. 16th, 1820
William Chandler and Lydia Seal[2]	3rd mo. 8th, 1821
William Cranston and Mary Johnson	4th mo. 12th, 1821
Charles Canby and Ann Richards[2]	10th mo. 11th, 1821
John Quinby and Elizabeth Phillips	6th mo. 6th, 1822
Henry Latimer and Sarah Ann Baily[2]	6th mo. 6th, 1822
Joshua Harlan and Ann Quinby	11th mo. 7th, 1822
James Webb and Lydia P. Richards[2]	11th mo. 14th, 1822
Henry Battin and Rachel Yarnall[2]	12th mo. 5th, 1822
David Wilson and Mary Poole[2]	5th mo. 8th, 1823
Simon Cranston and Hannah Cope[2]	5th mo. 15th, 1823
William Marot and Deborah Bassett[2]	3rd mo. 4th, 1824
John W. Tatum and Mary Canby[2]	6th mo. 10th, 1824
Stephen M. Stapler and Elizabeth Robinson[2]	6th mo. 17th, 1824
Joseph Ballance, Jr. and Mary L. Betts[2]	11th mo. 4th, 1824
William Richards and Lydia Seal[2]	12th mo. 9th, 1824
Samuel P. Johnson and Mary Ann Cranston	3rd mo. 10th, 1825
Richard Clement and Frances Canby[2]	5th mo. 18th, 1826
William Marshall and Margaret McCamon[2]	11th mo. 9th, 1826
Samuel Buzby and Maria Tatum[2]	3rd mo. 8th, 1827

Joel Fisher and Mary Brooks[2]	5th mo. 10th, 1827
John Clark and Ann Harlan	10th mo. 4th, 1827
John Bancroft, Jr. and Susanna Brookes[2]	6th mo. 12th, 1828
Ezra Hoopes and Ann Warner[2]	6th mo. 4th, 1829
Joseph Bancroft and Sarah Poole[2]	6th mo. 25th, 1829
Thomas Garret, Jr. and Rachel Mendenhall[2]	1st mo. 7th, 1830
Edward Grubb and Elizabeth P. Seal[2]	5th mo. 6th, 1830
Merrit Canby and Eliza T. Sipple[3]	5th mo. 20th, 1830
Jesse Mendinhall and Sarah R. Stroud[2]	11th mo. 4th, 1830
Thomas Baynes and Sarah Wetherald[2]	11th mo. 8th, 1832
Henry Gibbons and Martha Poole[2]	5th mo. 9th, 1833
William E. George and Hannah Poole[2]	5th mo. 23rd, 1833
Isaac Pyle and Ann Stern[3]	8th mo. 8th, 1833
Jacob Balderston and Ruth Ann Dawson[3]	5th mo. 13th, 1834
William S. Poole and Lydea Mendinhall[2]	12th mo. 11th, 1834
Abner Chalfant and Mary W. Betts[2]	4th mo. 9th, 1835
William Hodgson, Jr. and Elizabeth Richardson[3]	5th mo. 14th, 1835
Benjamin Ferris and Hannah Gibbons[2]	10th mo. 15th, 1835
Harlan Baker and Hannah Eastburn	12th mo. 10th, 1835
Jeremiah Hartley and Elizabeth Wetherald[2]	6th mo. 9th, 1836
Thomas Stapler and Sarah Webb[3]	12th mo. 7th, 1837
James A. Wright and Martha Tatum[2]	6th mo. 7th, 1838
William Kite and Mary F. Clement[3]	11th mo. 8th, 1838
Alban Buckingham and Mary E. Feanes	2nd mo. 6th, 1839
Albert M. Smith and Elizabeth Wollaston[2]	6th mo. 6th, 1839
Ellwood Garrett and Catharine K. Wollaston[2]	6th mo. 6th, 1839
Lindley Smyth and Elizabeth S. Ferris[2]	10th mo. 3rd, 1839
Lloyd Oakford and Rachel Wilkinson[2]	10th mo. 10th, 1839
Henry H. Paschall and Mary Anna Dixon[2]	12th mo. 3rd, 1840
Joseph Tatnall and Sarah Richardson[3]	6th mo. 10th, 1841
Edward C. Hewes and Sarah S. Garrett[2]	9th mo. 9th, 1841
Samuel Richardson and Susanna Robinson[2]	10th mo. 14th, 1841
Norris W. Palmer and Mary Webb[3]	4th mo. 7th, 1842
Joshua L. Pusey and Sarah W. Pyle[3]	9th mo. 8th, 1842
Joseph Bringhurst and Anna Richardson	10th mo. 6th, 1842
Moses Brinton and Margaret Ann Hallowell	3rd mo. 9th, 1843
Charles Warner and Mary R. Richardson	6th mo. 22nd, 1843
Charles W. Howland and Gulielma Maria Hilles[3]	9th mo. 7th, 1843
William P. Woodward and Rachel England[3]	1st mo. 4th, 1844
Joshua T. Heald and Hannah Pusey	4th mo. 18th, 1844
Jesse T. Bonsall and Mary Ann England[3]	5th mo. 9th, 1844
George S. Grubb and Mary T. Seal	5th mo. 23rd, 1844
Edward Tatnall, Jr. and Rachel R. Webb[3]	9th mo. 12th, 1844
Benjamin Poultney and Eliza Ellicott[3]	10th mo. 8th, 1844
Ellis P. Wilkinson and Sarah R. Cranston	12th mo. 4th, 1844
William Ferris and Mary Wetherald, Jr.	1st mo. 2nd, 1845
Henry Drinker and Frances C. Morton[3]	6th mo. 5th, 1845
Aron Hewes and Hannah Wollaston	7th mo. 3rd, 1845

Nathaniel Wilkinson and Mary Woodward	12th mo. 4th, 1845
William Canby and Ann Tatnall[3]	4th mo. 13th, 1846
Henry Garrett and Catharine Ann Canby	5th mo. 7th, 1846
John C. Deacon and Maria W. Buzby[3]	9th mo. 17th, 1846
Daniel Corbit and Mary C. Wilson[3]	4th mo. 15th, 1847
William C. Smyth and Emily Betts	9th mo. 28th, 1847
Joseph Davis and Elizabeth M. Peart	8th mo. 31st, 1848
Frederick Paxson and Lydia Betts	12th mo. 6th, 1848
Caleb Hood and Mary E. Hallowell	3rd mo. 8th, 1849
Clement H. Smith and Mary C. Emlen[3]	4th mo. 12th, 1849
William Sellers and Mary Ferris	4th mo. 19th, 1849
William R. Bullock and Elizabeth A. Emlen[3]	10th mo. 17th, 1850
Joseph Z. Lippincott and Elizabeth C. Tatum	10th mo. 31st, 1850
Samuel B. Regester and Mary S. Denny	11th mo. 26th, 1850
Edward Betts and Mary R. Tatnall[3]	9th mo. 25th, 1851
William Pyle and Margaret C. Painter	9th mo. 30th, 1851
Evan Thomas Swayne and Sarah W. Pusey	11th mo. 6th, 1851
John R. Tatum and Lucy Richardson[3]	4th mo. 15th, 1852
Samuel S. Downing and Mary Stapler[3]	5th mo. 27th, 1852
Jacob Heald and Sarah Ann Tyson	10th mo. 7th, 1852
Samuel N. Pusey and Mary T. Richards	6th mo. 9th, 1853
Joshua Hoopes and Rachel Bassett	11th mo. 9th, 1853
Joseph C. Turnpenny and Elizabeth Richardson	11th mo. 9th, 1853
Thomas Clarkson Taylor and Elizabeth S. Mendinhall	7th mo. 12th, 1854
Edward Askew and Rachel A. Conard	3rd mo. 8th, 1855
Edward T. Bellah and Sarah T. Richardson	1st mo. 24th, 1856
George S. Grubb and Lucretia R. Dixon	5th mo. 5th, 1856
William Ellis and Mary Fisher	10th mo. 26th, 1860
Samuel Loyd and Sarah P. Croasdale	2nd mo. 14th, 1861
Reuben Satterthwaite and Margaret A. Stapler[3]	3rd mo. 14th, 1861
Elliston P. Morris and Martha Canby[3]	3rd mo. 21st, 1861
Ferris Bringhurst and Mary N. Betts	12th mo. 5th, 1861
James England and Sarah Stroud[3]	5th mo. 14th, 1863
Granville Worrell and Mary S. Mendinhall	5th mo. 20th, 1863
David C. Woodward and Mary Stroud[3]	11th mo. 17th, 1864
Samuel Bancroft, Jr. and Mary A. Richardson	6th mo. 8th, 1865
John Sellers Bancroft and Eliz. H. Richardson	10th mo. 25th, 1866
Thomas Wistar and Mary Richardson[3]	6th mo. 27th, 1867
Daniel H. Kent and Mary Elizabeth Pusey	10th mo. 17th, 1867
Linton Smith and Margaret R. Warner	4th mo. 22nd, 1868
Charles Hallowell and Fanny Ferris	6th mo. 11th, 1868
Samuel D. Paschall and Hettie R. Grubb	9th mo. 16th, 1868
Robert P. Brown and Mary R. Tatnall[3]	10th mo. 15th, 1868
John R. Bringhurst and Elizabeth Tatnall[3]	2nd mo. 17th, 1870
Daniel W. Taylor and Mary P. Heald	4th mo. 6th, 1870
Jacob Pusey, Jr. and Jane Richardson	10th mo. 13th, 1870
J. Sellers Bancroft and Anne S. Richardson	9th mo. 27th, 1871
Isaac H. Shearman and Susan W. Hilles[3]	12th mo. 14th, 1871

William P. Webb and Laura Worrell	4th mo. 16th, 1872
Edward Bettle and Elizabeth H. Tatnall[3]	9th mo. 26th, 1872
George Gilbert Cameron and Lucy J. Richardson	10th mo. 8th, 1872
William B. Harrison and Agnes Garrett	5th mo. 20th, 1873
Alfred D. Warner and Emalea Pusey	4th mo. 30th, 1873
Frank T. Webb and Mary A. Pusey	5th mo. 4th, 1876
Lindley C. Kent and Anna Grubb	5th mo. 16th, 1876
William C. Malone and Mary A. Downing[3]	8th mo. 24th, 1876
Eldridge C. Price and Mary H. Ferris	10th mo. ——— 1877
W. Harold Smith and Isabella P. Sellers	1st mo. 30th, 1878
George Maclean and Mary J. Bancroft	6th mo. 20th, 1878
T. Elwood Marshall and Ellen S. Good	11th mo. 3rd, 1880
Frank H. Thomas and Phebe T. Chambers	10th mo. 6th, 1881
T. Chalkley Bartram and Anna P. Wollaston	11th mo. 16th, 1881
Calvin T. Bye and Isabell Pyle	4th mo. 19th, 1882
William Penn Evans and Mary Tatum[3]	9th mo. 28th, 1882
Willard Child and Emily Garrett	11th mo. 23rd, 1882
John J. Satterthwait and Lucy Heald	6th mo. 6th, 1883
Charles P. Blackburn and Deborah Ferris, Jr.	10th mo. 13th, 1886
David W. Masters and Catharine W. Garrett	10th mo. 21st, 1886
William C. Philips and Harriet L. Caldwell	11th mo. 17th, 1886
William A. Gawthrop and Frances A. Tanguy	4th mo. 11th, 1888
Frederick H. Robinson and Sarah Richardson Mendinhall	9th mo. 19th, 1888
Howard Sellers and Sarah Mendinhall Worrell	10th mo. 18th, 1888
Abraham Francis Huston and Alice Calley	1st mo. 17th, 1889
George A. Rhoads and Frances C. Tatum[3]	6th mo. 19th, 1890
Geo. Roaldson Thompson and Albina Gregg Philips	12th mo. 11th, 1890
John M. Mendinhall and Fanny J. Pusey	1st mo. 21st, 1891
Stirling Hibberd Thomas and Edith Needles Trump	10th mo. 11th, 1894
Charles Ross Mace and Susan Newbold Van Trump	11th mo. 14th, 1894
J. Newlin Gawthrop and Rebecca A. Pyle	11th mo. 21st, 1894
C. Linnaeus Lamborn and Ann Amanda Taylor	4th mo. 4th, 1895
David Jones Reinhardt and Anna Margaret Hewes[2]	6th mo. 30th, 1896
Robert R. Tatnall and Elizabeth Rhoads[3]	7th mo. 2nd, 1896
Walter S. Taylor and Helen Savery[3]	10th mo. 28th, 1897
John Richardson, Jr. and Eleanor Wilson Mendinhall	11th mo. 3rd, 1897
Arthur Kirkbridge Taylor and Rebecca Robb	11th mo. 10th, 1897
Eugene Martin Chambers and Sarah Snowden Rumford	6th mo. 23rd, 1898
Edward Mendinhall Philips and Bertha Cranston	12th mo. 1st, 1899
Roger Clark and Sarah Bancroft	6th mo. 18th, 1900
David Moore Hillegas and Anna Jenkins Mifflin	1st mo. 27th, 1904
Lindley C. Kent and Rosamond Beverly Chambers	6th mo. 22nd, 1904
Henry Goodman McComb and Margaret Irene Pierson	10th mo. 12th, 1905
Oliver Wilson Eastburn and Marian Ellen Evans[2]	6th mo. 21st, 1906
Henry Tregelles Gillett and Lucy Bancroft	3rd mo. 30th, 1908

Harry James Walter and Elsie Janney Way	1st mo.	7th,	1909
George Lodge Ewart and Hanna Mitchell Passmore	10th mo.	9th,	1912
Samuel Newbold van Trump and Mabel Bellingham Pierson	12th mo.	6th,	1912
Clarence A. Lane and Mary R. Downing[2]	11th mo.	1st,	1913
Charles Cyrus Speakman and Juliette Canby Van Trump	10th mo.	23rd,	1915
Wendell George McNees and Helen Mary Bye[2]	11th mo.	6th,	1915
Cyrus Stanley Chambers and Esther Kent Smedley	6th mo.	24th,	1916
Robert H. Maris and Katharine E. Spear[4]	6th mo.	15th,	1917
John Randall Arnold and Eugenia Ridgely	8th mo.	11th,	1917
Frank Williams Moore and Rachel Wilson Philips	7th mo.	12th,	1919
Earl Rankin Hitchcock and Helen Elizabeth Scott[2]	6th mo.	4th,	1920
Roger Pennock and Mary Wistar Tatnall[4]	6th mo.	19th,	1920
Pusey Passmore and Dora May McKee	10th mo.	16th,	1920
William C. Philips and Carolien Chambers Turner[2]	1st mo.	8th,	1921
Malcolm Acker Brosius and May Dewey Whittaker[2]	9th mo.	10th,	1921
Paul Van Amringe Comey and Elizabeth Kirk Eves	12th mo.	17th,	1921
A. Stanley Ayers and Margery Stapler	6th mo.	1st,	1922
Frederic Lawrence Pyle and Juliet Canby Mace[2]	9th mo.	9th,	1922
Edward Needles Trump and Rosamond Chambers Kent	2nd mo.	10th,	1923
Aylmer A. Robinson and A. Louise Philips	10th mo.	6th,	1923
Henry Dearden and Susan Marion Craig[4]	12th mo.	22nd,	1923
Thomas S. Carswell and Louise W. Thompson	3rd mo.	22nd,	1924
Robert H. Richie and Rebecca E. Hallett[4]	6th mo.	23rd,	1925
Joseph M. Beatty, Jr. and Elizabeth T. Rhoads[2]	6th mo.	4th,	1927
James Charles Tily and Marjorie Mode[2]	6th mo.	25th,	1927
Theodore Howell Pyle and Mary Marian Miller[2]	8th mo.	7th,	1928
Arthur Silver and Marion Rhoads[4]	6th mo.	15th,	1929
Chalmers Van A. Pittman and Margaret E. Hallett[4]	8th mo.	10th,	1929
Sergei A. Evreinoff and Frances R. Tatnall[4]	1st mo.	31st,	1931
Geoffrey Crowther and Margaret Worth	2nd mo.	9th,	1932
James H. Young and Evelyn S. Gane[2]	6th mo.	18th,	1932
Charles J. Darlington and Eleanor Collins	6th mo.	25th,	1932
Joseph McFarland, Jr. and Eleanor Rhoads	12th mo.	31st,	1932
Weston Holt Blake and Anne Hillborn Philips	3rd mo.	16th,	1934
George Alfred Perera and Anna Paxson Rhoads	12th mo.	22nd,	1934
Shermer Haines Stradley, Jr. and Margaret Elizabeth Spencer	7th mo.	1st,	1935
Louis Sloan Bringhurst and Ann Phoebe Walker	6th mo.	26th,	1936
Francis Marion Henley and Helen Ruth Philips	10th mo.	29th,	1937
Newlin P. Palmer and Eleanor Jarrett Penrose	6th mo.	7th,	1938

GENEALOGIES

Miriam Worrell Webb

BRINGHURST

I.   Joseph Bringhurst, a physician, came to Wilmington in 1793 from Philadelphia; m. 1799 Deborah Ferris. He was a great friend of John Dickinson.

II.   A son of Joseph, Joseph II, m. 1842 Anna Richardson.

II.   Another son, Edward, m. 1832 Sarah Shipley.

II.   A daughter, Mary Dickinson Bringhurst, m. 1842 George Vernon Moody.

CANBY

I.   Thomas Canby from Yorkshire, England, settled as a miller in Bucks County, Pennsylvania. In 1709 he married Mary Oliver.

II.   One of Thomas' sons, Oliver, came to Wilmington in 1740 and built the first flour mill on the Brandywine. His farm included the present "Bishopstead" property. In 1744 he married Elizabeth Shipley.

III.   A son of Oliver, William, m. 1747 Martha Marriott; and another son, Samuel, m. 1775 Frances Lea. Samuel Canby built for himself a "large and commodious house" at what is now Fourteenth and Market Streets, where he entertained many traveling Friends.

IV.   A daughter of William, Fanny, m. 1804 Benjamin Ferris; and another daughter, Anna, m. 1815 David Smyth.

V.   A son of Anna Canby Smyth, Clement B., m. 1856 Sarah Sellers.

IV.   A son of Samuel, James, m. 1803 Elizabeth Roberts.

V.   A son of James, Samuel II, m. 1832 Elizabeth C. Morris.

IV.   A daughter of Samuel, Esther, m. 1813 Josiah Clement.

V.   A daughter of Esther Canby Clement, Mary Foster Clement.

IV.   A daughter of Samuel, Elizabeth, m. 1796 John Biddle.

V.   A daughter of Elizabeth Canby Biddle, Frances, m. 1827 Thomas C. Garrett.

IV.   A daughter of Samuel, Mary, m. 1824 John W. Tatum.

CRANSTON

I.   Simon Cranston (1768-1856) son of William Cranston and Elizabeth (Meales) Bond, m. Mary Marshall, daughter of William and Mary Tatnall Marshall.

II.   A daughter of Simon, Mary Ann, m. 1825 Samuel P. Johnson. (See Johnson).

II. A son of Simon, James, m. 1836 Eleanor Armstrong.

FERRIS

I. Samuel Ferris came from near London, England, to Groton, Massachusetts, and later settled in New Milford, Connecticut. In 1682 he married Sarah Reed.

II. One of their sons, David, married Mary Massey and in 1748 settled in Wilmington, Delaware.

III. One of David's sons, Ziba, m. 1769 Edith Sharpless.

IV. Ziba had three children, Deborah, m. 1799 Joseph Bringhurst; Benjamin, m. 1804 (1) Fanny Canby, (2) 1835 Hannah Gibbons; Ziba II, m. 1816 Eliza Megear.

V. Deborah Ferris Bringhurst had three children, Joseph, m. 1842 Anna Richardson; Edward, m. 1832 Sarah Shipley; Mary, m. 1842 George Vernon Moody.

V. A son of Benjamin Ferris, David, m. 1849 Sarah Underwood.

V. Another son, William, m. 1845 Mary Wetherald.

V. Another son, Edward, m. 1855 Katherine Ashmead.

V. A daughter of Ziba II, Elizabeth, m. 1839 Lindley Smyth.

V. Another daughter, Mary, m. 1849 William Sellers.

GARRETT

I. Thomas Garrett, the great abolitionist, (1789-1871) from Upper Darby, Pennsylvania, came to Wilmington in 1822; m. (1) Mary Sharpless, (2) 1830 Rachel Mendinhall.

II. Children of Thomas and Mary Sharpless Garrett: Ellwood, m. 1839 Katherine Wollaston; Henry, m. Katherine Canby.

II. Son of Thomas and Rachel Mendinhall Garrett, Eli, m. 1855 Frances Sellers.

HOLLINGSWORTH

I. Valentine Hollingsworth from County Armagh, Ireland, m. (1) 1655 Ann Ree, (2) 1672 Ann Calvert.

II. A son of Valentine, Valentine II, m. 1713 Elizabeth Heald.

III. A son of Valentine II, James, m. 1747 Mary——.

IV. A son of James, Abner, m. 1788 Phoebe Hall.

V. A son of Abner, Abner II, m. Louisiana Kay.

JOHNSON

I. Robert Johnson and his wife, Margaret (Braithwaite), presented in 1714 a certificate from Carlow Monthly Meeting in County Wicklow, Ireland, to Newark

Monthly Meeting at Center. He with other Irish immigrants purchased plantations at Stenning Manor, now New Garden township.

II. A son of Robert, Joshua, came from Ireland with his parents, m. 1724 Sarah Miller and settled at Stenning Manor.

III. A son of Joshua, Robert II, m. 1762 a widow, Mary (Chambers) Wollaston.

IV. A son of Robert II, Joshua II, m. 1792 Ann Pennock.

V. A son of Joshua II, Samuel P., m. 1825 Mary Ann Cranston.

LAMBORN

I. Robert Lamborn, m. 1722 Sarah Swayne. He came to Chester County, Pennsylvania, from Berkshire, England, in 1713.

II. Robert's son, Robert II, m. 1746 Ann Bourne.

II. Another son of Robert I, Thomas, m. 1762 Dinah Carson (daughter of Richard and Martha Carson, members of Wilmington Meeting in 1738).

III. A daughter of Robert II, Susanna, m. 1768 John Marshall.

III. Another daughter, Sarah, m. 1783 James Webb.

IV. A son of Susanna Lamborn Marshall, Robert, m. 1804 Mary Hoopes.

V. A son of Robert Marshall, John, m. 1827 Malinda Worthington.

VI. One of the daughters of John Marshall, Lydia, m. 1858 Edward Mendinhall.

IV. One daughter of Sarah Lamborn Webb, Ann, m. 1808 Isaac Pyle.

IV. Another daughter of Sarah Lamborn Webb, Sarah, m. 1837 Thomas Stapler.

V. A daughter of Ann Webb Pyle, Sarah Pusey.

III. One of the sons of Thomas Lamborn, Jonathan, came to Wilmington from Upper Oxford, m. (1) 1805 Rachel Moore, (2) 1818 Martha Squibb.

IV. One of Jonathan Lamborn's daughters, Miriam, m. 1833 Thomas Worrell.

V. One of Miriam Lamborn Worrell's five children, Emma, the teacher.

LEA

I. John Lea, m. 1698 a widow, Hannah (Hopton) Webb and came in 1699 on the "Canterbury" to Pennsylvania from Wiltshire, England. He was a minister among Friends and frequently made religious visits to distant parts. He died in Springfield, Pennsylvania.

II. Children of John: Isaac, m. 1721 at Christ Church, Philadelphia, Sarah Fawcett, and moved to Wilmington in 1751; Hannah, m. 1726 Joseph Bonsall; John II, m. (1) Hannah Edge, (2) a widow, Mary (Yarnall) Pennell.

III. A son of Isaac, James, m. 1741 Margaret Marshall.

IV. A daughter of James, Elizabeth, m. 1765 Joseph Tatnall.

V. A daughter of Elizabeth Lea Tatnall, Ann, m. 1794 Thomas Sipple.

V.   A daughter of Elizabeth Lea Tatnall, Esther, m. 1798 William Warner.

VI.   Sons of Esther Tatnall Warner: Charles Warner and Edward Tatnall Warner.

V.   A son of Elizabeth Lea Tatnall, Edward, m. 1809 Margery Paxson.

VI.   Children of Edward Tatnall: Elizabeth, Joseph, Sarah, Joseph, Edward, Thomas, William, Anne, Margaret, Mary, Henry, Lea, Margery.

IV.   A daughter of James Lea, Frances, m. 1775 Samuel Canby.

IV.   A son of James Lea, James, Jr., m. 1781 Elizabeth Gibson.

V.   A daughter of Frances Lea Canby, Esther, m. 1813 Josiah Clement.

VI.   A daughter of Esther Canby Clement, Mary Foster Clement.

V.   A daughter of Frances Lea Canby, Elizabeth, m. 1796 John Biddle.

VI.   A daughter of Elizabeth Canby Biddle, Frances, m. 1827 Thomas C. Garrett.

VII.   A daughter of Frances Biddle Garrett, Rebecca, m. 1856 Jonathan Rhoads.

V.   A daughter of Frances Lea Canby, Mary, m. 1824, John W. Tatum.

III.   A daughter of John Lea II, Hannah, m. (1) 1772 Joseph Canby, (2) 1782 Joshua Pusey, Jr.

IV.   A son of Hannah Lea Pusey, Jonas, m. 1811 Hannah Pennock.

V.   A son of Jonas Pusey, Joshua III, m. 1842 Sarah W. Pyle.

IV.   Another son of Hannah Lea Pusey, Jacob, m. (1) 1813 Hannah Nichols, (2) 1818 Hannah Mendenhall, (3) 1841 Louisa Webster.

V.   A son of Jacob Pusey, Lea, m. 1847 Ann Kersey.

V.   Another son of Jacob Pusey, Joseph M., m. Elizabeth Philips.

PASCHALL

I.   Thomas Paschall, m. 1665 Joanna Sloper.   He came to America in 1681.

II.   A son, Thomas II, m. (1) 1692 Margaret Jenkins, (2) Abigail (Fowler) Golding.

III.   A son of Thomas II, John, m. 1728 Frances Hodge.

IV.   A son of John, Henry, m. 1770 (1) Anne Garrett, (2) Ann Lincoln.   Both Henry and his father were doctors.

V.   A son of Henry, John II, m. 1806 Sarah Horne.

VI.   A daughter of Henry, Margaret, m. Samuel Hadly Dixon; and a son, Henry Paschall II, m. 1840 Mary Anna Dixon.   (Both Samuel Hadly Dixon and Mary Anna Dixon were children of John Dixon and Mary Shipley).

POOLE

I.   William Poole from Cumberland, England, m. Jeannott Twentyman.

II.   A son of William, Joseph, b. 1704, m. Rebecca Janney.

III. A son of Joseph, William II, b. 1728, m. Elizabeth Shipley Canby.

IV. A son of William II, William III, b. 1764, m. Sarah Sharpless.

V. Children of William Poole III: Elizabeth P. Sellers, b. 1792; Rebecca Poole, b. 1793; Mary P. Wilson, b. 1795; Samuel Poole, b. 1796; Hannah P. George, b. 1798; William S. Poole, b. 1801; Sarah P. Bancroft, b. 1804; Martha P. Gibbons, b. 1807; Anna P. Hallowell, b. 1810; John Morton Poole, b. 1812.

RICHARDSON

I. John Richardson from Lincolnshire, England, sailed on the ship, "Endeavor," and settled in New Castle, in 1682. "In 1705 due to his political and civic influence, a plot of ground was purchased and a Quaker meeting-house built." m. Elizabeth ——.

II. John Richardson II, second son of John I, came to this country with his parents and settled on the banks of the Christiana Creek. The Newark meeting frequently met at his house. He married in 1704 Ann Ashton and had 12 children.

III. A son of John II, Robert, m. 1750 Sarah Shipley.

III. A daughter of John II, Susannah, m. 1710 Peter Bayard.

III. Another daughter of John II, Jane, b. 1727, m. Dr. John McKinly, first president of Delaware.

III. A son of John II, Richard, m. 1766 Sarah Tatnall.

IV. A son of Richard, Joseph, m. 1803 Ann Spackman.

V. A son of Joseph Richardson, Samuel, m. 1841 Susanna Robinson.

IV. A son of Richard, John III, m. 1813 Margaret Paxson.

V. A son of John III, John IV, m. 1856 Martha Andrews.

V. Another son of John III, Joseph P., m. 1856 Sarah Andrews. (Martha and Sarah Andrews were both daughters of Mary and John Andrews).

ROBINSON

I. Francis Robinson from County Wicklow, Ireland, settled in New Castle County, m. Elizabeth ——. In 1672 he was a witness to the marriage of Valentine Hollingsworth in Ireland.

II. A son of Francis, Nicholas, chief burgess of Wilmington, m. 1750 Mary Hicklin.

III. A son of Nicholas, William, m. 1764 Elizabeth Hanson.

IV. A daughter of William, Susanna, m. 1841 Samuel Spackman Richardson.

SHIPLEY

I. William Shipley from Leicestershire, England, came to Wilmington from Ridley, Pennsylvania. While in England he was married to Mary Tatnall; and after her death to Elizabeth Levis of Pennsylvania in 1728.

II. Children of William and Mary (Tatnall) Shipley: Thomas, b. 1718, m.

Mary Marriott; Ann, m. Joseph Maris; Elizabeth, m. (1) 1744 Oliver Canby, (2) 1761 William Poole; Mary.

II.   Children of William Shipley and his second wife Elizabeth: Sarah, m. 1750 Robert Richardson; William, m. Sarah Rumford.

III.   A son of Thomas Shipley, Joseph, b. 1752, m. Mary Levis.   A daughter, Sara, b. 1755, m. Cyrus Newlin.

III.   A son of Elizabeth Shipley and Oliver Canby, William Canby, m. 1747 Martha Marriott.

III.   Another son of Elizabeth Shipley Canby, Samuel Canby, m. Fanny Lea and a daughter, Mary, m. Abraham Gibbons.

III.   A son of Elizabeth Shipley and her second husband, William Poole, William, m. 1791 Sarah Sharpless.   Quotation from an old family chart: "They had one child who was well worth the cost of raising."

III.   Children of Sarah Shipley and Robert Richardson: John Richardson; Elizabeth Wharton; Mary; Ann Latimer.

IV.   A son of Joseph Shipley, Joseph II, b. 1795, was one of the founders of Brown, Shipley and Company after having been in the counting-house of Samuel Canby, Philadelphia.

IV.   A son of Joseph Shipley, Samuel, m. Elizabeth Jefferis.

V.   A daughter of Samuel, Sarah Shipley, m. 1832 Edward Bringhurst.

SMITH

I.   Samuel Smith, (1794-1861) m. Sarah Watson.   He came from Philadelphia to Wilmington where he was head of a school at Third and West Streets.

II.   A son of Samuel, Albert, m. 1839 Elizabeth Wollaston.

STAPLER

I.   John Stapler, m. 1720 Esther Canby.

II.   One of their children, Thomas, m. 1750 Rachel Atkinson.

III.   A son of Thomas, William, m. 1780 Mary Mitchell.

IV.   A son of William, Stephen, m. 1824 Elizabeth Robinson.   (See West family).

IV.   Another son, Thomas, m. 1837 Sarah Webb.

TATNALL

I.   Ann, widow of Robert Tatnall of Leicestershire, England, came to America in 1725.

II.   A son of Robert and Ann Tatnall, Edward, m. 1735 Elizabeth Pennock and moved to Wilmington soon after his marriage.

III.   A son of Edward Tatnall, Joseph, m. (1) 1765 Elizabeth Lea, (2) Sarah

Paxson. Joseph Tatnall was a miller and also largely interested in the shipping trade. He built his home at 1803 Market Street.

IV. Children of Joseph: Sarah, b. 1765, m. Thomas Lea; Margaret, b. 1767, m. James Price; Elizabeth, b. 1770, m. Joseph Baily; Edward; Ann, b. 1775, m. John Bellah; Joseph died in 1798 of yellow fever; Esther, b. 1779, m. William Warner; Edward, m. 1809 Margery Paxson; Thomas died in 1798 of yellow fever.

V. Children of Edward Tatnall: Joseph, Edward, William, Henry L., Elizabeth Gillis, Sarah Febiger, Anne T. Canby, Mary Betts, Margery Warner.

WEST

I. Thomas West, uncle of Benjamin West the painter, m. 1709 Mary Dean. He was from Bucks, England, and was at one time burgess of Wilmington.

II. A daughter of Thomas and Mary West, Elinor, m. 1742 James Robinson.

III. A son of Elinor West Robinson, Thomas, m. 1787 Mary Wilson.

IV. A daughter of Thomas Robinson, Elizabeth, m. 1824 Stephen Stapler.

V. A daughter of Elizabeth Robinson Stapler, Mary, m. 1852 Samuel F. Downing.

BURIALS IN THE MEETING YARD

Margery Stapler Ayers

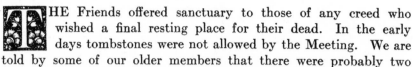HE Friends offered sanctuary to those of any creed who wished a final resting place for their dead. In the early days tombstones were not allowed by the Meeting. We are told by some of our older members that there were probably two thousand burials before the first burial permit was issued in 1824. As nine hundred ninety-one permits were issued, nearly three thousand persons must have been buried in the graveyard. There are records of one thousand one hundred sixty-two burials, only a few of which were before 1808. During one of the great plagues, a trench was dug on the Fifth Street side of the yard, extending toward West Street, in which the victims were buried.

In the following list the names of those who were members of the Society of Friends are marked with an asterisk.

Abbott (child of Cyrus)..........1825	Baddy, Hannah E...............1862
Abbott (child of Cyrus)..........1828	Bailey (wife of Edw. T.).........1829
Abbott (child of Cyrus)..........1830	Bailey, Edward T...............1843
Abbott (child of Cyrus)..........1832	*Bailey, Elizabeth................1808
Abbott, Sarah..................1832	*Bailey, Elizabeth................1841
*Adams, Susan Hanson...........1866	Bailey, Jeremiah................1847
Adams, Susan H................1866	Bailey, Joseph..................1843
*Alderdice, Jane................1835	Baker, Mary E.................1826
*Alderdice, Ruth................1853	*Baldwin, Elizabeth.............1816
Allen, Caroline.................1836	*Baldwin, Hannah...............1811
Allen, Elizabeth................1837	*Baldwin, Joseph................1811
Allen, Henry...................1837	*Baldwin, Lydia.................1817
Allen, Samuel..................1839	*Bancroft, Edward..............1839
Allen, Sarah Elizabeth..........1811	*Bancroft, Joseph...............1874
*Allen, Sarah...................1887	*Bancroft, Sarah P.............1896
Allen, Wm. Franklin............1842	*Bancroft, Susan...............1838
*Alrichs, Jacob.................1857	*Bane, Elizabeth................1815
*Alrichs, Lydia.................1825	*Bane, Margaret................1834
*Alrichs, Mary Ann.............1812	*Bane, Nathan, Jr..............1816
*Alrichs, William...............1823	*Bane, Nathan.................1817
*Alsop, Anna...................1849	*Barker, Sarah.................1837
Antrim (child of Pinder).........1815	Barr, Ellen Jane................1835
*Ashbornham, Rachel...........1822	*Bassett, Ann..................1862
Ashburnham, Elizabeth.........1868	*Bassett, Elizabeth.............1890
Askew, Anna Mary.............1841	*Bassett, Hannah...............1810
*Askew, Hannah................1851	*Bassett, Nathan...............1847
Askew (child of Doc. H. F.)......1832	*Bassett, Ruth.................1873
*Askew, Parker................1834	*Bassett, Sarah................1826
Askew, Samuel.................1842	*Baynes, Fanny................1837
*Awmack, Mary................1828	*Beeson, Elizabeth.............1823

Carpenter, William............1828
Cason, Joseph.................1825
Cathcart, George..............1848
Chalfont, Mary W..............1836
Chandler, Joseph..............1831
*Chandler, Lydia..............1842
*Chandler, Phebe..............1841
Chandler, Sarah...............1834
Chandler (child of Wm.)........1824
Chandler (child of Wm.)........1826
Chandler (child of Wm.)........1830
Chandler (child of Wm.)........1830
Chapman, Benjamin.............1827
Chapman, Esther Ann...........1828
*Churchman, Hannah J..........1882
Churchman, Micayah............1856
*Clark, Amelia H..............1838
*Clark, Ann...................1851
Clark, Eleanor................1824
*Clark, John..................1854
Clark (child of Thos.).........1824
Clayton, Caleb................1835
*Clement, Edward S............1837
Clement (child of Josiah).......1830
Clement, Josiah F. C..........1833
Cloud, Mabel..................1854
*Cloud, Susanna...............1809
Collins, George...............1851
Comfort, Charles..............1835
Comfort, Edmund...............1838
Comfort, Elizabeth............1836
Comfort (child of Ezra)........1824
*Comfort (child of Ezra).......1831
Comfort (child of Ezra)........1842
*Comly (child of Ann).........1858
*Comly, Ann...................1858
*Commons, Hannah..............1813
*Conard, Anthony..............1885
*Connard, Rachel Ann..........1874
*Conway, Ann..................1861
*Cooper, Caleb S..............1863
Cooper, Caroline..............1827
Cooper, Josiah................1864
*Corse, Rebecca...............1864
*Corse, Sarah Ann.............1887
*Corse, Susan Cassandra........1889
*Covington, Hannah............1857
Craig (child of David).........1842
Craig, Elizabeth..............1828
Craig, Frederick..............1841
*Craig, Mary..................1839
*Croasdale, Stevenson..........1867
*Curl, Mary...................1838
Curtis, Mary and child.........1832

Davis, Agnes E................1882
Davis, Charles................1861
Davis, George.................1865
Davis, Harry G................1874

Davis (child of Jason).........1861
Davis (child of Jason).........1868
Davis (child of Jason).........1868
Davis (child of Jason).........1869
Davis, William................1862
*Dawson, Elizabeth............1836
Deacon, Elizabeth.............1850
Deacon, Gilbert...............1836
Deacon (child of Stacy)........1851
*Denny, Ann...................1845
Denny (child of Chas.).........1832
Dickinson, David..............1825
Dickinson, John...............1808
Dickinson, Mary...............1803
*Dixon, Amy...................1825
*Dixon, Edwin.................1828
*Dixon, Elizabeth.............1834
*Dixon, Isaac.................1816
*Dixon, John..................1822
*Dixon, Margaret..............1830
*Dixon, Mary..................1844
Dorsey, Lydia.................1843
Dorsey (child of Wm.)..........1829
*Downing, Mary Ann............1832
Duncan, Emma..................1840
Duncan, Mary B................1837

*Edge, Sarah Ann..............1857
*Edwards, Agnes...............1864
*Edwards, Charles F...........1849
Edwards, Edward...............1858
*Edwards, Edward..............1875
*Edwards, Harriet.............1849
Edwards, Joseph...............1872
Edwards, Sarah M..............1847
*Egan, Mary P.................1875
*Elliott, Harvey..............1840
Ellis, Benjamin...............1825
Ellis, Sarah Ann..............1824
*Emmerson, Lydia..............1849
England, J. Clemson...........1837
England (child of Lewis E.).....1832
*Erwin (child of Jno.).........1825
Erwin, Sarah..................1826
Evans (child of Jno.)..........1825
Evans, Marian.................1839
Evans, Nathan.................1854
Evans, Thomas.................1826

Faddus, Hetty Ann.............1839
Faddus, Magdalina.............1836
*Ferris, Ann..................1822
*Ferris, Anna.................1814
*Ferris, Anna M...............1890
*Ferris, Benjamin, Jr.........1831
*Ferris, Benjamin.............1867
Ferris, Catherine L...........1916
*Ferris, David................1908
*Ferris, Deborah..............1897

*Ferris, Edith................1815
Ferris, Edward...............1919
*Ferris, Eliza M..............1880
*Ferris, Fanny................1833
*Ferris, Frances..............1838
*Ferris, Francis..............1843
*Ferris, Francis C............1880
*Ferris, Hannah...............1767
*Ferris, Hannah...............1860
*Ferris, John.................1828
*Ferris, Joseph W.............1858
Ferris, Katherine L...........1916
*Ferris, Martha...............1912
*Ferris, Mary W...............1907
*Ferris, Matilda..............1937
*Ferris, Phoebe...............1832
*Ferris, Sarah................1869
Ferris, Sarah A...............1891
Ferris, Thomas M..............1916
Ferris, William...............1909
*Ferris, William Canby........1928
*Ferris, Wm. Megear...........1819
*Ferris, Ziba.................1794
*Ferris, Ziba.................1875
Fincher, Barkley C............1839
Fincher, Catherine............1838
Fincher, Sarah................1835
Fincher, William..............1834
Fincher, William..............1838
*Ford, Abraham................1832
Ford, Abraham.................1833
Ford, Benjamin................1827
*Ford, Frances................1812
Ford (child of Isaac).........1825
Ford (child of Isaac).........1826
Ford (child of Isaac).........1827
Ford (child of Isaac).........1832
*Ford, Mary...................1814
Ford, Samuel..................1841
Ford, William, Jr.............1833
*Ford, William................1847
Fothergill, Alexander.........1843
*Fothergill, Mary.............1854
Frankelbury, George...........1825
*Fredd, Mary..................1854
Freize, Mary Ann..............1824
*Fussle, Esther...............1815

*Gardner, Adeline.............1836
Garrett, Eli..................1874
*Garrett, Mary................1828
*Garrett, Rachel..............1868
*Garrett, Thomas..............1871
Garrettson, Elizabeth.........1852
Garrettson, Rebecca M.........1852
*Garrison, William............1808
*Gibbons, Mary................1876
*Gibbons, Rebecca Jr..........1837
*Gibbons, William.............1845

Giffin (child of John)........1829
Giffin (child of John)........1830
Giffin (child of John)........1831
Giffing, Harriet..............1850
Giffing, John.................1828
Giffing, Thomas R.............1855
*Gilpin, Abigail..............1815
Gilpin, Ann...................1840
*Gilpin, Edward...............1844
Gilpin, Eugene................1835
*Gilpin, Hannah...............1841
Gilpin, Joseph R..............1824
Gilpin, Lewis.................1840
*Gilpin, Lydia................1831
Gilpin, William...............1843
Gilpin, William W.............1827
*Godwin, Sopha P. L...........1833
Gould (child of Jos.).........1836
Gould, Margaret Ann...........1839
Graham, Isaac G...............1834
Graham, Simeon Batton.........1834
*Grassell, Susanna............1848
*Graves, Edmund...............1848
*Graves, Edward...............1848
*Graves, Maria................1849
*Graves, Mary A...............1896
*Graves, Robert J.............1848
*Graves, Robert M.............1890
Gray, Ann.....................1824
Gray, Eliza Jane..............1824
Gray, Welcome.................1846
Gregg, Elizabeth..............1844
Gregg, George.................1835
Gregg, John...................1825
Gregg, Mary...................1813
Gregg, Sarah..................1846
Griffith, Jane................1812
Groome, Joseph................1841
Groome, Sarah Ann.............1844
*Grubb, Edward................1845
*Grubb, Hester................1833
*Grubb (child of Jos.)........1810
*Grubb, Joseph................1830
*Grubb, Samuel S..............1830
*Grubb, Sarah.................1824

Hadden, Susan.................1848
*Hallowell, Anna P............1896
*Hallowell, Benjamin S........1874
*Hallowell, George P..........1814
*Hallowell, Jane..............1854
*Hallowell, Jesse.............1873
Hallowell, Wise...............1834
Hamilton, Rachel..............1825
Hamilton, Susannah............1828
Hampton, Ann..................1848
Hampton, Edward H.............1848
Hance, Ann Jane...............1838
Hance, Elizabeth..............1838

*Hanson, John P	1812	*Hewes, Sally	1853
*Hanson, Mary	1827	*Hewes, Wm. Henry	1827
*Hanson, Samuel T	1812	Heyburn, Elizabeth	1851
*Hanson, Susannah	1813	Heyburn, George	1833
*Hanson, Thomas	1819	Hickman, Wm. Jr	1836
*Hanson, Wm. Savory	1814	*Hill, Amy S	1864
Harlan, Leah	1867	*Hill, John, Jr	1851
*Harlan, William	1819	*Hilles, Edward	1813
Harris, Barnabas	1825	*Hilles, Eli	1863
Harris, Margaret	1829	Hilles, Eli, Jr	1893
*Hart, Hannah	1830	*Hilles, Elizabeth B	1907
Hartley, Amanda	1853	Hilles, Kate	1859
*Hartley, Ann	1848	*Hilles, Martha	1849
Hartley, Benjamin	1856	*Hilles, William	1811
Hartley, David	1872	Hilles, William B	1867
Hartley, Edward	1837	*Hilles, William P	1859
Hartley, Edward	1843	*Hirons, Elizabeth	1831
Hartley (child of David	1847	*Hirons, John	1829
Hartley, Henry C	1848	Hirons (child of John)	1831
*Hartley, Joseph	1849	Hirons, Thomas M	1831
*Hartley, Margaretta	1885	Hollingsworth (child of Achilles)	1834
*Hartley, Martha	1829	Hollingsworth, Franklin	1841
Hartley, Mary Ellen	1849	Hollingsworth, Henry	1840
*Hartley, Milton	1848	*Hollingsworth, Jesse	1843
*Hartley, Phebe	1824	Hollingsworth, John W	1841
*Hartley, Phebe	1832	*Hollingsworth, Mary E	1837
Hartley, Phebe	1846	Hollingsworth, Thomas	1829
*Hartley, Ruth Ann	1891	*Hallowell, Mary	1819
Hartly, Sally Ann	1834	*Hallowell, Mary Pierce	1819
*Harvey, Job	1816	*Hoopes, Ann W	1886
Harvey, Sally Ann	1847	*Hoopes (child of Ezra)	1830
Harvey, Townsend	1841	Hoopes, Ezra	1855
Harvey, William	1832	Hoopes, Martha	1839
Hayes, John	1842	Hoopes, Sarah Ann	1839
Hayes (child of Jos. Jr.)	1841	Hughes, Mary	1825
Hayes, Rachel	1813	*Hull, Phebe	1817
Hayes, Sarah	1824	Hurmer	1831
Hayes, Sarah	1840	*Hurnard, Lucy	1820
Hayes (wife of Stephen)	1828	Husbands, John	1833
Hayes, Stephen	1830	Huston, Ann	1839
*Hayhurst, Margaretta	1838	*Huston, Drusilla	1888
*Hayhurst, Martha B	1836	Huston, John A	1851
Hays, Samuel	1825	Huston, Mark B	1869
Heald, Benson Henry	1826	Huston, Sarah	1832
Heald, Henry	1829	Hutton, Elizabeth	1841
Heald, Margery	1826	*Hutton, Pierce	1841
Heald, Samuel	1826	*Hyatt, Thomas	1838
*Hedges, Hannah	1829		
*Henry, Amelia	1847	Jackson, Ann	1828
Hepburn, George	1833	Jackson, Anthony Wayne	1849
*Hewes, Aaron	1866	*Jackson, Dinah	1821
*Hewes, Ann	1834	Jackson, Garnet	1849
*Hewes, Deborah	1838	Jackson, Martha H	1849
*Hewes, Edward	1826	Jackson, S. J	1869
Hewes, Ellis	1831	*James, Joseph	1837
*Hewes, Hannah	1863	Jeanes, Mary	1841
*Hewes, Hannah C	1844	Jefferis, Bazilal	1847
*Hewes, Mary	1830	Jefferis, Charity	1836
*Hewes, Orpha	1840	Jefferis, Charles	1850

Miller, Ann B................1887
Miller, Elizabeth.............1829
Miller, Hannah................1829
Miller (child of Isaac)..........1825
Miller (child of Isaac)..........1828
Miller, Mary.................1829
*Miller, Mary................1838
Miller, Orpha................1832
*Miller, Rebecca..............1846
Minick, William...............1826
*Mitchell (wife of John)..........1823
*Mitchell, John...............1826
Moody, Geo. V., Jr............1847
Moody, Mary D...............1886
*Moore, Elizabeth.............1858
Moore, George................1842
Moore, Henry................1857
Moore, John.................1843
*Moore, John C...............1834
Moore, Joshua H..............1843
*Moore, Mary................1870
Moore, Thomas...............1852
Morris, Elizabeth.............1830
*Morris, Elizabeth B...........1860
Morrow (child of John)..........1831
*Morton, Margaret.............1852
Mulford, Isaac I..............1844

Nemdall, Ruth................1830
Newlin, Charity...............1833
*Newlin, Cyrus...............1824
Newlin (child of Cyrus)..........1830
Newlin (child of Cyrus)..........1830
Newlin (child of Cyrus)..........1832
Newlin (child of Cyrus)..........1833
Newlin (child of Cyrus)..........1838
Newlin (a child)..............1841
Newlin, Hannah...............1833
Newlin, Joseph...............1842
*Newlin, Sarah...............1824
Newlin, Sarah................1833
Newlin (child of Thomas).......1831
Newlin, Thomas..............1838
*Nichols, Eliza...............1816
*Nichols, Hannah.............1825
*Nichols, Lydia...............1816
*Nichols, Margaret............1865
*Nichols, Ruth...............1841
*Nichols, Samuel.............1817
Niles, Hezekiah..............1839

*Oakford, Henry A............1857
Oakford, Mary W.............1849
Oakford, Rachel W............1850
Otley, Abner................1827

*Painter, Phebe..............1866
Painter, Samuel..............1829
Painter, William.............1851

Palmer, Elizabeth.............1832
Palmer, Maria...............1836
Palmer (child of Moses).........1828
Palmer (child of Norris)........1827
Palmer, Norris...............1842
*Palmer, Sarah...............1828
Palmer, William..............1831
Parker, Rebecca Connell........1836
Parker, William Thomas........1838
*Parmer (child of Moses)........1823
Passmore, Joanna.............1825
Passmore, Mary..............1845
*Paynter, William.............1854
Pearce, Anna................1852
Pearce, Ann Matilda...........1860
Pearson, George..............1838
Pearson, Joseph..............1830
Peirce, Dinah................1828
Peirce, Rebecca..............1844
Pierce, Celie................1840
Pierce, Elizabeth D............1876
Pierson, George..............1836
Pierson, Rebecca.............1827
Pierson, Robert..............1840
Pierson, William.............1832
Pierson, William Henry.........1828
Pierson (child of Wilson)........1832
Pierson (child of Wilson)........1837
Pierson (child of Wilson)........1838
Pierson (child of Wilson)........1839
*Platt, Alice................1806
Platt (2 children of John).......1826
Platt (child of John)...........1834
Plumline, Bridget.............1850
Plumline, John...............1846
Plumline, Sarah..............1835
Plumline, Thomas.............1845
*Poole, Edward...............1838
*Poole, Jane................1839
*Poole, Lydia................1844
Poole, Margaret..............1857
*Poole, Mary M..............1837
Poole, Myra E...............1854
*Poole, Sally Ann.............1828
Poole, Samuel L..............1870
*Poole, Sarah................1823
*Poole, William..............1829
*Poole, William..............1846
*Poole, William S.............1857
Poultny, Ann................1862
Price, James, Jr..............1832
Price, James................1840
Price (child of John)...........1837
*Price, Margaret.............1841
*Price, Rhoda...............1825
*Pusey, Hannah..............1837
*Pusey, Jane Richardson........1918
Pusey, Lea.................1839
*Pusey, Sarah Ann............1828

Seal, Sarah T	1873	Smith (child of M. and A.)	1829
Seal (child of Thomas)	1826	Smith, Mary	1835
*Seal, William	1842	*Smyth, Anna Canby	1867
Sebborn, James	1825	*Smyth, David	1866
*Seeds, Adam	1823	Smyth, Ferris	1843
*Seeds, Allice	1823	*Smyth, Lucy	1890
Seeds, Sarah Elizabeth	1837	*Smyth, Mary Anna	1897
Sellers, Frances F	1859	*Smyth, Sarah M	1826
Shalcross, Isaac	1832	*Souy, Naomi	1840
*Shallcross, John	1831	*Souy, William R	1840
Sharp, Sabilla Ann	1836	*Spackman, Thomazin	1832
Sharp, Susan	1828	*Speakman, Edith	1847
Sharpless, Mary	1812	Speakman, Phebe	1842
*Sheward, Caleb	1817	Speakman, Thomas	1846
Sheward, Caleb B	1863	Spencer, John	1826
Sheward, Isaac G	1859	Spencer, Mary Ann	1855
Sheward, Percy	1828	Springer, Charles	1843
*Sheward, Rest	1816	Springer, Dallas	1848
Sheward (child of Wm.)	1837	Springer, Elizabeth	1858
*Shipley, Anna	1852	Springer, Franklin	1845
Shipley, Edwin	1861	Springer, Hannah	1850
*Shipley, Elizabeth	1883	Springer, Henry	1847
*Shipley, Elizabeth	1867	Springer (child of Samuel)	1846
*Shipley, Elizabeth L	1866	Springer, Samuel	1853
*Shipley, Hannah	1891	Springer, Victorine	1857
Shipley, Henry	1861	*Squibb, Catharine	1833
Shipley, Hester	1852	*Squibb, Ellen B	1831
*Shipley, Jane	1808	*Squibb, Mary H	1831
Shipley, John	1824	Squibb, Nathaniel	1841
Shipley, John	1862	*Squibb, Rachel	1836
Shipley, Joseph	1829	*Squibb, Robert	1828
*Shipley, Joseph	1832	*Squibb, Sarah	1831
Shipley, Joseph	1867	*Squibb, Thomas	1835
*Shipley, Mary	1843	Stanton, Elizabeth	1841
Shipley, Orpha	1843	*Stapler, Ann	1847
Shipley, Robert	1834	*Stapler, Ann B	1837
Shipley, Samuel	1848	*Stapler, Hannah Ann	1839
*Shipley, Sarah	1857	*Stapler, Sarah	1865
*Shipley, Sarah	1872	*Stapler, Stephen M	1855
*Shipley, Thomas	1813	*Stapler, Thomas	1820
Shipley, Thomas	1824	Starr, Amanda	1851
Shipley, Thomas	1856	*Starr, Aquilla	1816
*Shipley, William	1816	Starr, Caleb	1851
Shipley, William	1829	Starr, Charles	1895
Shipley (child of Wm.)	1831	Starr, Edward G	1890
Shoemaker, William Henry	1864	Starr, Elizabeth W	1864
Sidebothan, Thomas, Jr	1843	Starr, Emily	1848
Simmons (child of C.)	1825	*Starr, Isaac, Sr	1811
Simmons, Charlotte	1835	Starr, Isaac	1849
Simmons (child of Geo.)	1832	*Starr, Isaac H	1849
Simmons, Mary	1875	*Starr, Jane	1812
Simmons, Sarah	1842	Starr, Joshua	1853
Simmons (child of Wm.)	1833	Starr, Joshua	1857
Simpson, Edward	1836	Starr, Lewis	1891
Skelton, James	1851	Starr, Mary	1828
Smith (child of A. and A.)	1828	Starr, Ruth	1892
*Smith, Grace	1808	Starr, Susannah	1828
Smith, Elizabeth	1836	Stidham, Jos. H	1870
Smith, John	1820	Stokeley, Charles	1830

*Stokeley, Esther..............1862
Story, Betty..................1827
Stringfellow, Jane............1845
*Stroud, Caleb.................1861
*Stroud, Elizabeth.............1813
*Stroud, Elizabeth.............1847
*Stroud, Elizabeth, Jr.........1869
*Stroud, Elizabeth.............1882
*Stroud, Esther................1843
*Stroud, Joshua................1834
Stroud (child of Joshua).......1845
Stroud (child of Joshua).......1846
Stroud, Joshua.................1862
Stroud, Lillie W...............1860
Stroud, Lucy...................1863
*Stroud, Martha................1833
*Stroud, Martha, Sr............1875
*Stroud, Mary B................1874
*Stroud, Samuel................1832
Stroud (child of Wm. and Jane)...1856
Swayne, Rebecca................1861
*Swayne, Susan.................1826

*Tatem, Mary C.................1833
*Tatim, David..................1822
*Tatnall, Joseph...............1813
*Tatnall, Margery..............1837
*Tatnall, Sarah................1828
*Tatum, Amy Y., Jr.............1863
*Tatum, Ann....................1834
*Tatum, Hepsiba................1840
*Tatum, John...................1818
*Tatum (child of John).........1826
Tatum, John W..................1866
*Tatum, Lydia..................1840
*Tatum, Mary...................1834
Taylor, Rachel.................1838
*Temple, Daniel................1856
*Thistlewaite, Ann.............1821
Thomas, Anna...................1845
Thomas, Charles................1850
*Thomas, Evan..................1825
Thompson, James................1846
*Torbert, Ellen................1856
Torbert, John..................1842
Torbert, Mary Jane.............1846
Townsend, Mary Ann.............1832
Townsend, Mary Ann.............1843
Tripp, John....................1833

Vaughn (child of Lydia)........1835
*Walker, Hannah S..............1846
*Walker, James.................1812
*Walker, Jane..................1853
Walker, William................1825
Walker, William................1835
Wall, Rebecca..................1844
Wallan, Willie C...............1862
*Walton, William C.............1862

Wardell, John..................1836
*Warner, Esther................1860
*Warner, Henry.................1845
*Warner, Mary..................1837
Warner, Victorine..............1839
*Warner, William, Jr...........1826
Warner, William................1845
Warrington, Elizabeth..........1828
*Way, Ann......................1809
*Way, Jane.....................1841
*Way, John.....................1833
*Way, Nicholas.................1822
*Wayne, Sarah..................1865
*Webb, Jacob...................1827
Webb, James....................1831
*Webb, Lydia...................1831
*Webb, Sarah Ann...............1839
*Webster, Eliza................1847
Webster, John..................1837
Webster, John..................1837
*Webster, Lydia................1809
Wells, Jane....................1825
Wells, Obed....................1825
*West, Mary....................1834
*Wetherald, Joseph, Jr.........1833
*Wetherald, Joseph.............1842
*Wetherald, Joseph.............1843
*Wetherald, Martha Havorth.....1824
*Wetherell, William............1840
*White, Ann....................1813
*White, Ann....................1822
*White, John...................1815
*White, John...................1829
*White, Joseph.................1815
White, Levi....................1824
*White, Mary...................1836
White, Ruth Ann................1849
*Whitelock, Martha.............1823
Whitelock, Mary................1836
Wier, Eleanor..................1855
Wiley, Alvin N.................1868
Wiley, Ann Eliza...............1846
Wiley, L.......................1836
*Wiley, Martha.................1828
*Wiley, Samuel.................1849
Wilkens (child of William).....1865
Wilkins (child of William).....1826
*Wilkinson, Ann................1853
*Wilkinson, Hannah.............1809
Wilkinson, Jane P..............1843
*Wilkinson, Mary...............1845
*Wilkinson, Rachel.............1852
*Wilkinson, Robert.............1815
*Wilkinson, Robert.............1856
Wilkinson, Thomas Evans........1844
Willdin, Sarah Ann.............1835
*Williamson, Alvina............1849
Williamson, Charles............1828
*Williamson, Harriot...........1821

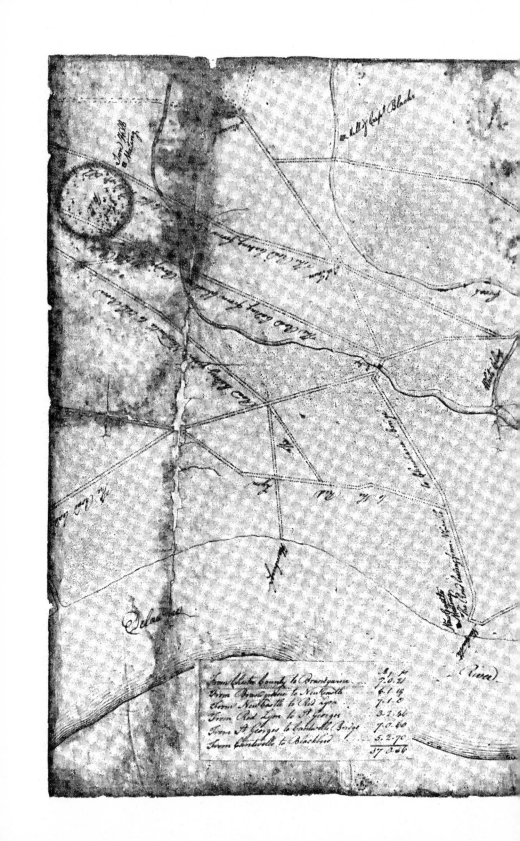

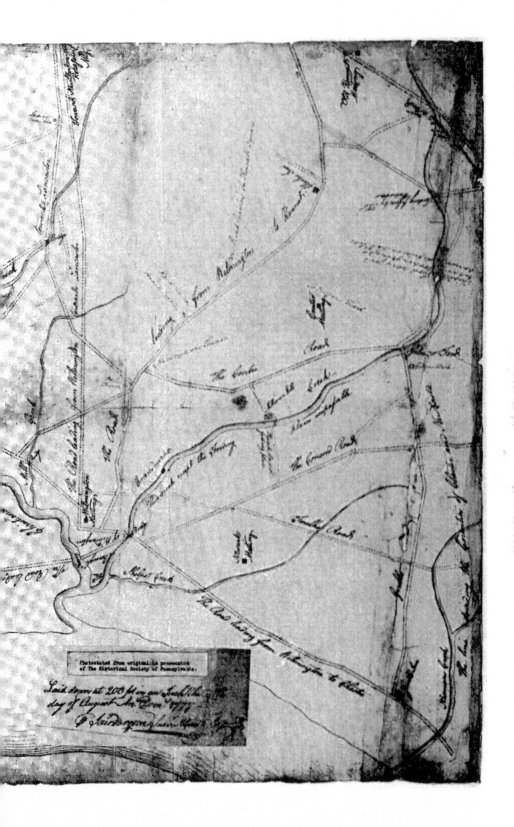

Chas. L. Story Company
Wilmington - Delaware

Made in the USA
Middletown, DE
06 March 2016